Mid-Life Issues
and the Workplace
of the 90s

Mid-Life Issues and the Workplace of the 90s

A Guide for Human Resource Specialists

SHIRLEY A. WASKEL

QUORUM BOOKS
New York • Westport, Connecticut • London

Library of Congress Cataloging-in-Publication Data

Waskel, Shirley.
  Mid-life issues and the workplace of the 90s : a guide for human
resource specialists / Shirley A. Waskel.
      p.   cm.
  Includes bibliographical references and index.
  ISBN 0–89930–619–5 (alk. paper)
  1. Age and employment—United States.   I. Title.   II. Title:
Midlife issues and the workplace of the 90s.
  HD6280.W37   1991
  331.3′94—dc20   90–26217

British Library Cataloguing in Publication Data is available.

Library of Congress Catalog Card Number: 90–26217
ISBN: 0–89930–619–5

First published in 1991

Quorum Books, 88 Post Road West, Westport, CT 06881
An imprint of Greenwood Publishing Group, Inc.

Printed in the United States of America

The paper used in this book complies with the
Permanent Paper Standard issued by the National
Information Standards Organization (Z39.48–1984).

10 9 8 7 6 5 4 3 2 1

This book is dedicated to the adult students and mid-life people who have shared their lives with me. Without their input, I would not have recognized, read about, and discussed, with them and others, these issues that are common to us all.

Contents

Preface

First and foremost, my gratitude goes to the people who throughout my life have provided encouragement, were willing to accept me where I was at the time, and empowered me to search more deeply. Without them, this book wouldn't have been possible.

I am fortunate to have a group of friends who were willing to share their talents in order to make this the best book possible. For the hours of discussion and for their thoughtful reading and editing, my thanks go to Judy Dierkheising, Louis Deily, and Judy Austin, who listened to me and provided information and a great deal of support. I want to express a special word of appreciation to David Hinton, who understands that each individual has special talents and ways to express them.

There are several tasks that can be boring, tedious, and seemingly without reward. Roxanne Owens performed one of these. She searched for the most current information, read and reread the materials, checked references, and performed so many other tasks. Margaret Dubes was willing to read the final version word by word and line by line. Her contributions have made this an easier book to read. A close relationship develops between the writer and the typist. I was fortunate to have a typist who insisted on perfection if at all possible. Edna Miller not only typed the manuscript but also pulled me back to the work when I was willing to say "that's enough." Her high standards enabled me to produce high-quality work.

Any errors or mistakes in the manuscript are mine.

A special thanks goes to Tom Gannon at Quorum Books, who gave me an avenue to put into print thoughts and ideas that seemed important to me.

Mid-Life Issues
and the Workplace
of the 90s

Introduction

The maturing workplace is now a reality. In fact, mid-life employees are becoming the subject of articles and books. There is a projected worker shortage for the end of the 1990s. We see advertisements begging older workers to reenter the work force and help serve others by taking a position at Burger King or McDonald's.

The U.S. Department of Labor issued its agenda, "Workforce Quality: A Challenge for the 1990s, Secretary Dole's Agenda for Action," to address the labor shortage, its causes and possible solutions. The society has made a shift toward a service-producing economy. There is more evidence that the work force is ill-equipped to meet the challenges of a global economy.

Since I began writing this book, there has been an increased number of articles that address these issues. The major emphasis has been on the lack of worker skills and the slow response rate of organizations, which hesitate to provide the necessary training. There is also the lack of concern on the part of companies for their employees' needs and desires. As buyouts, mergers, closings, and obsolete skills continue within the work force, more mid-life workers are either forced or choose to leave. Rapid change and the scramble to become competitive within a global market economy require well-trained, skilled, intelligent, and experienced workers. Paradoxically, these are the very workers who are encouraged to leave the work force. Organizations do not capitalize on the positive aspects of mid-life workers. Instead they use attractive packages to propel these workers from a productive work life into early retirement. It is also not uncommon for mid-life workers to find their jobs boring or dissatisfying. This comes at a time when mid-life workers are reaching their peak potential. Those who have continued to learn and grow both personally and on the job are eager for the challenges of the twenty-first century. They recognize the changes that are happening around them. Mid-life men who have worked their entire lives now have reexamined their early dreams of young adulthood and have established more realistic goals. They have accepted and adjusted to the fact that upward mobility in the work force has given way to lateral moves. Many have already proven themselves and want to escape from the rat race of bigger and better. They are interested in quality.

Mid-life women are entering the work force in greater numbers. Many have returned to complete their education and now have the necessary skills. Often the move toward work is prompted by economics. There are children who cannot accumulate enough money to attend college. Husbands may be reaching their peak salary level. The cost of living is rising. There are thoughts of having sufficient money for the retirement years. Women also return to the work force for their own sense of self. They are no longer involved in raising the children. They have recognized that they are responsible for their own sense of self and continued growth. These are middle- and upper-middle-class issues and responses. There are those men and women who have held low-paying jobs because of a lack of skills, training, or education. They continue in the work force as a matter of necessity. They know that they must continue to work to survive financially. They too have dreams of having more input or responsibility on the job. Some, because of their inability to achieve this, do the job to make the money necessary to have the things they need and want. Some become obsolete and are unable to continue working because they do not have the skills necessary in this technologically advanced world of work.

Mid-life workers are finding that their life expectancy is increasing and that they enjoy better health than their predecessors. As a result, new issues continue to surface that need to be addressed. Until recently, business and industry have offered retraining. Mid-life employees could not take or have not taken advantage of the opportunity. Continuously working until a later age will become more of a need as well as an option. Mid-life people who take advantage of early retirement may find themselves in the position of wanting to reenter the work force at a later age. Others may find themselves displaced and will need upgrading and retraining in order to be employable in another track. These are some of the differences that make up the new workplace picture. Other issues that influence mid-life workers are also gaining prominence. Workers value their input regarding reward systems, economic security, and job design. They are reassessing their job responsibility and employee benefits, including employee assistance programs.

Automation and new technology, changing working conditions, and changing products and jobs need to be addressed in new ways. The current concept of literacy needs to include computers and other modern technology. There is an influx of material available on dysfunctional and addictive behaviors. This enables workers to be more aware of what they want and need in order to function productively within the work force. Many employees are less willing to work within dysfunctional organizations. They are more knowledgeable about their own behaviors and are more aware of being responsible for their own mental health. As a result, they are asking for more support services within the work force as well as within the community. Employers need to be aware of a wide range of personal and human resource specialists' policies that affect the maturing work force. These include positive personnel techniques that facilitate the organizational development necessary to recruit, retrain, and manage mature workers effectively. Jobs and the work environment need to be redesigned. A consideration of criteria that take into account the physical capabilities and limitations of mid-life workers is required.

Continuous education is gaining recognition as a must within organizations. A team approach provides an avenue for imparting new knowledge, developing new skills, and creating new job opportunities. It is now possible with the new technology to tailor jobs to fit employees.

A study by the American Society of Personnel Administration and the Commerce Clearing House shows that 66 percent of those who responded identified types of training techniques that could be used most successfully. Examples include self-paced learning, experiential training, on-the-job coaching, application-oriented training, and training in which the workers themselves participate in the design as the most effective ways of teaching new skills to the maturing worker. It is also becoming more apparent that unless the goals of the organization and the goals of the workers match, neither group's goals will be met. This will be problematic.

Other problems arise as well. There are those mid-life workers who have personal problems that carry over to the job. Many workers are not aware that their behavior causes problems for those with whom they work. There are those who are addicted to chemicals, food, or gambling or who exhibit other obsessive or compulsive behavior. These problems can affect the president of the company down through the maintenance person. Depending on the extent of the problem and the philosophy of the organization, these workers could be fired, promoted, demoted, or ignored. Whatever way they are regarded, their behavior does affect others within the organization and the organization as a whole.

There are mid-life workers who are codependent as well. They also cause problems. These are the people who seem to be so willing to do whatever is asked of them but either blatantly or subtly cause problems. They create and foster triangles causing people to be at odds with one another. Or they may overfunction. They do everyone's job, including or perhaps excluding their own. They eventually burn out. There are those who underfunction. They let Joe do it. They have been used to having someone rescue them at the drop of a hat. These are people with problems. The problems can be addressed. A great many of these people can, through proper counseling, become healthy, functioning workers. As a human resource specialist, you are called on to deal with all types of people within your organization. It is helpful for you to know that although mid-life has its ups and downs, there are people who are available to address those problems that are beyond the scope of your job and your ability.

Those workers who are considered to be mid-life are becoming a larger portion of the work force. They are the people that businesses and organizations will need to depend on through the twenty-first century. They are the thirty-five-year-olds who are beginning to address the developmental tasks of mid-life. They are the forty-five-year-olds who have completed some of those tasks but are recognizing other areas they need to address. They are the fifty-year-olds who are beginning to realize that their life is probably more than half over. They are starting to ask themselves what they want and how they want to spend the rest of their lives. Since people are living longer and are in better health, chronological age has become the last effective measure of one's age. Therefore, there are even fifty-five- to sixty-year-olds who still describe themselves as in mid-life. These people have much to contribute, but they also have to deal with the myths and stereotypes that still exist regarding older people. Society and they themselves might be in a struggle between how they feel and how others view them.

An increase in interest about mid-life issues has become evident to me. During the past ten years I have taught a course that includes a look at mid-life and career change issues. Students of all ages and from a wide variety of disciplines have taken this course. Because of the increased interest in and knowledge on human behavior, major course changes take place about every three years. Mid-life career change was talked about ten years ago, but very few people were interested. Over the years more mid-life people have begun to express interest. These include students who have raised families and now want to enter the work force and those who have been in the work force since early adulthood and now want to change careers. There are some who recognize that either their behavior or that of their coworkers is less than positive.

Although these students are familiar with terms like *addictive behavior* and *dysfunctional organizations*, they still know very little about how each affects them. They sense it, but they are not able to describe or recognize characteristics. As a result, they know they need to make changes but are at a loss as to what changes need to be made. The students do not know how to initiate these changes or where to seek the help they need. There are reading and media materials available, but they are scattered and represent varying degrees of value. The point is that just because the information is out there does not mean that individuals are using it.

For example, yesterday I received a call from a mid-life career woman who has worked in the health care field her entire career. Her major responsibility is training and development. She is pursuing a doctorate and called to seek information about the mid-life course. During the conversation, she mentioned that one of her interests is second careers for mid-life people. She indicated that she had recently read an article addressing this concept. It was new to her, and she wanted to investigate this further. This is not unusual. Somewhere between preparing for a career and working within that career a void seems to build. I suspect part of it results from the concentration on getting specific tasks accomplished, leaving little time for reading, thinking, dreaming, and recreating.

This is probably the best explanation of the driving force behind this particular book. As an educator, I feel strongly that current information needs to be presented in a variety of ways. Most of what you will read here probably isn't new to you. The way it is organized and presented may offer you another way of looking at it. In the end, it may be that a teacher teaches what the teacher needs to learn. I am also sure that each of you who reads these pages will have insights, understandings, and examples that either complement the writing or provide a strong case against what has been written. I welcome all your responses and reactions. Unless we are confronted with new ideas, with different ways of looking at information and its impact on the world, we become stale and out-of-date.

Just a word of caution: When you discover different ways of looking at human behavior, you gain insight into why people act as they do, and you thus commit to changing the world. There is the risk that you may want to do more than you are qualified to do and attempt to be more than you can be to others. Examine your needs and motives before you try to rescue employees from themselves. The purpose of this book is to give information and broaden your understanding on a variety of topics. Unless you are trained in counseling, you will be better served to refer employees to those who are. You can empower, teach, develop, and prepare better programs and learning situations. You can be an intermediary between employees and employers. In light of these thoughts and reflections, let us move on to a brief overview of the chapters you will be reading.

Chapter 1, "The Maturing Work Force," will explore the issues that affect mid-life workers. One of the major changes has occurred in the rapid advancement of technology. Younger members of the work force have grown up with computers, word processors, computer games, and other examples of this technological world. For mid-life workers, these advancements mean change, adaptation, and sometimes work skills obsolescence. As a result, businesses can identify a cadre of inadequately trained people. Often, outdated work skills are not the fault of the mid-life worker. Businesses hire younger workers and invest their training money to keep these workers current. Mid-life workers are often viewed as having a limited work life. Sometimes they fall between the cracks. Because of the impending worker shortage rising from a dearth of younger people and the increase in numbers of mid-life workers, employers will need to rely on this group to provide their work force needs. As businesses begin to explore and reevaluate their mid-life work force, they will become aware of how valuable these workers are. It may come down to a simple matter of economics.

The U.S. government has already recognized that unless mid-life workers are attended to, the business community will lose. As the country moves from a manufacturing to a service economy, new job skills are being identified. To provide the necessary training and to change attitudes among workers, the society will need to become a learning society. It is no longer sufficient to have completed a number of years of schooling. People need to continue to learn throughout their lives so that they can continue to be productive employees, as well as grow personally.

As a human resource specialist, you encounter and will continue to encounter mid-life workers who have problems, including addictions and shaming behaviors that occurred in childhood and have not been resolved. Dysfunctional family systems take their toll in the workplace as well.

Chapter 2, "Why People Act as They Do," provides some insights to you about people who cause problems within the workplace. Often, these problems are a result of unresolved issues from childhood and young adulthood. You will learn more about codependency, addictive behaviors, shame-based people, and the issues that can result from these dysfunctional behaviors. You will read short vignettes that explore the information within a personal context. Throughout the book, examples are given that are based in reality. Names, places, and situations have been changed to protect the privacy of the individuals involved.

Chapter 3, "Family Issues as They Relate to the Work Force," looks at problems that exist within families and how those problems can play a part in the workplace. Historically, the workplace was looked on as a second family. This was encouraged by employers and sought out by employees. At times, this can be positive. Teamwork and team building can thrive when employers and employees have common goals and objectives. There seems to be more evidence that work life and home life are not as separate as once thought. On the other hand, if workers grew up in dysfunctional families and have not come to terms with their own problems, the family-type workplace can mirror the family of origin. Unresolved issues will be played out within the work environment. These can prove disastrous for both the company and the employee. Although many will feel the burden of this behavior, it falls to the human resource specialist to address the resulting issues and problems. Although you are not by profession a counselor, you will need to identify dysfunctional behaviors. It will then be to your advantage to refer people with unresolved issues and problems to the appropriate sources.

Chapter 4, "Mid-Life, a Time of Change," explores the issues and changes that result from the developmental tasks common to mid-life. Several theories that seem most appropriate within the mid-life worker context will be presented. Several of the major tasks of mid-life will be explored. Among the most common are coping with the losses that occur in this stage of life, addressing the health issues, and coming to terms with the concept of mortality. Restructuring the dream is a mandatory task that is often ignored or overlooked. Self-assessment is important for people to be able to move through mid-life and continue to mature successfully. For those who are at the latter stages of mid-life, the concept of generativity is of great importance. Throughout their lives, people experience transitions. Because of the nature and the process of transition, people often think they are losing their minds, acting in a crazy manner, and they are often viewed by others as having "lost it." Actually, a transition is a normal process that has three components: an ending, a neutral zone, and a beginning. Each of these components can be troublesome if the individual involved does not understand the normalcy of the transition plus the need to complete each component before moving on.

As work and personal life become more integrated, organizations will find that they can provide services that will increase their employees' productivity and mental health. Human resource specialists will find that employee assistance programs (EAPs) can be very beneficial and can provide services that are not available within many organizations.

Chapter 5, "The Dysfunctional Workplace," explores both dysfunctional organizations and their effect on those who work there. Since it is accepted that there are dysfunctional people within society, it stands to reason that some of those people own and operate businesses. If the owner or the chairman of the board is dysfunctional, the rules governing the organization will include elements of this type of behavior. It is more difficult for employees to deal with problems within their work environment when people at the top operate out of their dysfunctional modality. It is possible that corporate leaders are healthy individuals but have hired middle managers who are dysfunctional. Workers again become caught in a situation over which they have little, if any, control. Workers themselves, as previously suggested, can be dysfunctional. Their fellow workers can appeal to healthy middle managers or corporate officers, often with positive results. If the organization operates from a closed system in which control is the major operational mode, there is almost no chance that resulting problems can be resolved. Healthy workers may find that the best way to deal with the problems is to resign and seek other employment. If this happens too frequently, the organization is left with those who are less than healthy themselves. If human resource specialists are employed in this type of organization, they find that they are not able to introduce or provide the kind of leadership they envisioned as part of their role.

Burnout is one of the results of working within dysfunctional organizations. Part of the problem is that these types of organizations have a public message and a private or internal agenda that clash. People are drawn to the organization because of the publicly established set of goals and objectives. Once hired, employees find that the organization operates from an entirely different set of rules and has another agenda in mind.

Another problem plaguing organizations is the need to lay off or terminate workers. Sometimes this is the result of advanced technology. It may also be due to changing needs within a global economy. Companies that are fighting to keep an edge in the rapidly changing workplace may have to cut back in order to stay financially sound. Human resource specialists are an important part of the layoff and termination process. Employees who find that they no longer have a job go through a grieving process. Part of themselves has been taken away. They can no longer identify themselves as someone who performs a particular task. Besides the financial burdens that result, their sense of self and their identities are affected. They are in need of outplacement services, at the very least.

Chapter 6, "Managers' Dilemmas," addresses the differences that exist between leadership styles and management. As more people become interested in learning more about themselves, they also begin to realize that what had seemed to be personality conflicts were actually style differences. When employees were viewed by their organizations as the means by which to complete the task at hand, they were treated differently. Today, as more people realize that they have more to contribute than just responding to someone else's orders, they are asking for more autonomy. This is especially true of mid-life workers. They are no longer content to do what they are told. They want to have a say and to make a contribution.

As companies reorganize to meet the needs and demands of a global economy, they will profit from looking more closely at their mid-life workers. These are the people who have learned through experience, have tested their ideas and seen other ideas tested. They know what will probably work and what is doomed to failure. Although younger workers bring to the organization a sense of adventure and a knowledge of what is new, they often lack the experience necessary to implement the ideas. They can learn from mid-life workers, who are at the stage in their lives where they can provide experience and insight.

Discrimination has always existed within the workplace, but employees are now more aware of what it entails. They are less willing to put up with discrimination toward themselves and others. Whereas everyone can say that racism does not belong in the workplace, everyone can cite instances. This is true of ageism as well. People can work longer and more effectively in this service-oriented economy. They are in better health, and jobs require less physical prowess than formerly. It is partly the organization's responsibility to aid older mid-life people from becoming obsolete. Sexual discrimination is more subtle and often more difficult to prove. Old myths and stereotypes about a woman's place are difficult to change. Attitudes toward women develop early in the maturation of individuals. These are so ingrained that when confronted, many people would deny having any negative attitudes. Yet these same people will not support or even try to underpin women's progress within the workplace. Mid-life women are beginning to recognize their worth. They are joining younger women in endeavoring to achieve equal pay for comparable work. Here again, human resource specialists have an important role to play. They need to be keenly aware of the intricacies of sex discrimination and sexual harassment.

Chapter 7, "Technology's Impact on the Workplace," concerns itself with the need for continuous, lifelong learning as a result of technological advances. Corporations are addressing this need through training programs. Human resource specialists need to be aware of the advantages and disadvantages of training by the corporation and by outside consulting firms. They are responsible for knowing what the needs of the corporation are, how the employees are qualified or not qualified to meet these needs, and what kind of training is necessary. One area that has been expanded is that of literacy. Previously, literacy was confined to the skills of reading, writing, and simple math. Today, the concept has been expanded to include computer skills.

Mid-life workers are a valuable asset because they are at a period in their development when they are eager to leave a legacy for the coming generations. One of the ways this can be accomplished is through mentoring. If human resource specialists understand the role and place of mentoring, they can utilize this process.

Anothern modern-day event that may cause problems in the not-too-distant future is early retirement. With a possible worker shortage on the horizon, older mid-life workers who are given the opportunity to retire early may be needed to complement the existing work force. Since early retirement policies will continue for the time being, it is beneficial to the corporation and the retiree to make that transition as easy as possible. The human resource specialist can provide a positive response that will do much for the company's image.

1

The Maturing Work Force: An Overview

Never in the history of this country has the changing nature of the work force elicited so much attention. For the first time there is serious talk of a maturing work force, a problem of inadequately trained people for the jobs available due to changes in technology, and a labor shortage.

Until recently the major developmental task for the mid-life employee was, "What will I do when I retire?" The work issues of mid-life people were limited to reevaluating the dream. It was time to redefine one's employment goals. On the other hand, if the employee was a problem, the problem was short-lived because the employee would soon be gone. Fellow workers would cover until then. If too many personal problems spilled over into the work environment, the worker could easily be replaced, usually by a less costly younger worker.

Human resource specialists had different concerns then. This has changed because of the aging of the work force and the continual changes brought on by technology, as well as the threat of a labor shortage. It is important to respond positively to the maturing members of the work force and their issues. Providing the insight and the means to overcome negative behaviors identified within the middle-aged work force will be more cost-effective than hiring and training new persons. This will become a greater priority as fewer younger people become available.

Who are these middle-aged workers? What are their characteristics? What are some of the problems peculiar to them? What issues do human resource specialists face? What are some possible responses?

ISSUES AFFECTING THE MATURING WORK FORCE

Individuals who are between the ages of thirty-five and fifty-five are defined as middle-aged. Included are the baby boomers, who will make up a substantial portion of workers in this age group.

According to Johnson and Packer (1987), the average age of the American worker will rise to thirty-nine by the year 2000. It is now thirty-six years. The U.S. Department of Labor predicts that by the year 2000, workers between the ages of thirty-five and fifty-four will increase by more than 25 million. This will represent just more than half (51 percent) of the total work force.

"The graying of America" will become a baby boomer's buzzword as the nation's middle-aged work force population swells to an all-time high. This age group will be a healthier and better-educated majority than ever before.

Historically, middle age was the time when workers began to consider their retirement options. They viewed themselves as working until age sixty-five and then, like those who had gone before, retiring. However, the last decade has seen more and more companies offering buy-out plans to people approaching late middle age. Oftentimes these plans are so attractive that workers feel compelled to accept them. The workers know that if they do not take the buy-out, they will eventually be let go. In fact, a new industry, outplacement counseling, has been created to respond to the needs of these workers.

For those not involved in buy-outs or early retirement, it is predicted that they will not be willing to seek other employment. They may not want to exert the time and energy necessary to adapt to major changes in their work life or personal life. In addition, dual-career families will be extremely cautious about any moves that might affect a spouse's career. This includes any type of move that would take them to another city or part of the country (Johnson & Packer, 1987).

Although the projection of multiple careers throughout one's lifetime has been around for quite a while, it was more of an idea than a reality. Establishing a second career has become more of a reality. When mid-life workers reach their peak of effectiveness or when they see their productivity leveling off, they realize that it is time to pause and reevaluate. There are several routes these people choose to follow. Those who respond by taking a deeper look into themselves use this time to gain a deeper understanding of self. They begin to self-actualize. They are the healthiest members of the work force. Unfortunately, those with unresolved issues may follow another road. Some will become miserable, while others will be less than productive. Others will do the minimum necessary to keep their jobs but will find no satisfaction. Another group will be constantly looking for other employment with or without the impetus to change jobs. It is these groups that will prove problematic for the human resource specialists (Thomas, 1982).

Technological Advancements

If middle-aged workers become more content to stay where they are, the advancements in technology will render many of them obsolete. Increased levels of education and training will be imperative to meet the demands of the 1990 work force. With fewer younger workers and less willingness on the part of the maturing work force to change, there will be fewer qualified people to fill the jobs created by this technological age.

In the past, changes occurred but not so rapidly. Usually society had a chance to catch up with one change before another one came barreling down. This is no longer the case. What was adequate yesterday no longer fits today. This rapid change can cause frustration and confusion. There is a tendency to dig in when the stress level becomes too high. Again, the person who is especially vulnerable is the middle-aged worker. Previously, anticipatory socialization taught these mid-life employees to prepare for retirement during their late middle-aged years. Now they are faced with making a major investment in upgrading their skills, searching for more acceptable employment, or staying at the same level for an undetermined number of years. All of this has come about because of the major changes caused by technological advancements.

Inadequately Trained People

Many entry-level jobs could conceivably require college degrees by the year 2000. In addition, the line between working and learning will blur in the future. Most workers will need some degree of retraining about every five years. Well-trained and experienced workers will become a high-priced commodity to business executives, schools, and organizations. Their training and retraining will be common and will often be at the company's or tax-payers' expense. As a result, employers will begin to see their workers in a new light. The labor force is increasingly being seen as an asset to be wooed and nurtured (Johnson & Packer, 1987).

An example of the change technology has made on the qualifications of its work force is reflected in a want ad for a floor sweeper. In the past, a person was qualified if the person could push a broom. The ad now asks for people who can operate electrical machinery as well as mix cleaning solutions and water. A floor sweeper must understand and be able to interact with an electrically driven machine and have a knowledge of mathematics. This calls for adequate reading skills that include comprehension of the directions to mix the chemicals used in cleaning.

Labor Shortage

Another major change looming large on the heels of the "early buy-outs" and continued early retirement is the predicted labor shortage. The tendency on the part of the employee to remain stable will impede a corporation's ability to respond quickly to change and opportunities.

From the employer's point of view, workers' demands will be perceived differently. There will be a shortage of younger workers willing to take the lead at much lower salaries. Those hired to replace mature employees will be expensive in a tight market. Additionally, the early retirement pay due the older worker will further strain the corporation's budget. Preretirement layoffs and "early outs" will be expensive options that companies will want to avoid. Middle-aged workers will want a greater involvement in decision making and more active participation.

The maturity factor that middle-aged employees can bring with them offers a more experienced and stable work force. This could increase productivity and efficiency as well as lighten the effects of a tight entry-level labor market. As the growth rate in this nation continues to slow to less than 1 percent, the pool of available workers will become more important. We have not experienced such an extreme dearth of workers since the years of the Great Depression (Johnson & Packer, 1987).

Valuable Workers

New middle-aged entries into the work force will provide yet another challenge to corporations as well as to human resource specialists. These nontraditional workers will want to enter the job market. They will also be at a disadvantage, since most of the new jobs will demand more education and higher levels of language, math, and reasoning skills. There are three major groups that will be affected most directly by these changes: disadvantaged workers, women, and minorities.

Disadvantaged Workers. The socioeconomically disadvantaged have historically been in the least advantageous position to improve their educational and skill levels. They will be least likely to meet the demand for highly skilled employees who can understand and utilize advanced technology. There will be a disparity between the skills required for a job and the skills that the disadvantaged bring with them to the job interview. They either will have to be trained and be willing to acquire such training or will fall seriously short of the requirements. This will become a grave economic issue for this nation as well as for those individuals who are able to do only manual or factory labor. The brawn necessary during the industrial revolution will be exchanged for brains during the 1990s (Gayle, 1990).

Mid-Life Women. Significant numbers of women in their forties and fifties, and even into their sixties are reentering the labor force after considerable time out. They often lack the experience and current job skills needed. The issues most commonly identified are escalating divorce rates, changing views concerning work and marriage, and maintaining or increasing the family's standard of living (U.S. Department of Labor, 1989).

The *Older Worker Task Force*, a report by the U.S. Department of Labor, indicates that several key questions have emerged regarding the increased reentry into the labor market by middle-aged women. Why do women leave the labor force and why do they return? What happens to women who seek employment after a period of absence from the labor force? How many experience unemployment? What types of jobs are available? What kind of wages do they obtain? What barriers do they face to reemployment?

The study discovered that women leave to rear children, to care for ailing or elderly family members, or to move to another location. Women return because of economic necessity: widowhood, divorce, or a husband's low earnings, disability, or unemployment.

There is a certain amount of stress that accompanies each of the reasons given for reentering the work force. This can prove to be problematic for the employee and the human resource specialist. In 1987, 10.4 percent of all women in their late thirties and forties were out of the labor force for an average of one month. They had entered by the following month.

Another long-standing problem is that wages paid reentry women are often lower than those paid continuous workers. Women were paid less originally, so when they reenter, they are still paid a low wage. This makes low wages a greater problem than wage loss. A labor shortage, however, should reduce the disparity between male and female pay.

By the year 2000, 47 percent of the work force will be women as the necessity for dual-income families will continue (Johnson & Packer, 1987). Also, women legitimately desire to work outside their homes to use hard-earned knowledge and expand their talents. Although women will continue to enter the work force at a high rate, they will want to work less (Deutsch, 1990). In a recent Gallup Poll, six out of ten working mothers wanted part-time employment (Johnson & Packer, 1987). Only half of those polled believed they could adequately fulfill responsibilities to both home and job by working full time. If the demands for more flexibility are not met by employers, many value-laden, middle-aged working women may choose to leave the labor market to care for children or to care for an older parent. This will further reduce the number of new or available workers in an already tight labor market.

Minority Workers. According to Johnson and Packer (1987), minorities are becoming a majority. About 29 percent of the work force will be non-whites by the year 2000. Immigration could add another 750,000 per year, counting legal and illegal aliens and their offspring over the next ten years. Like women, minorities of all ages will be entering the work force. They will come with their own unique set of problems, including different cultural norms and varying levels of education and trainability. Previously, it was expected that lower-status minorities would take the low-tech jobs. But as the technology increases, so does the need for literacy and basic computational skill. This will leave many low-income mid-life minorities unable to respond to training. As a result, they will be unemployable.

WHY HUMAN RESOURCE SPECIALISTS WILL WANT TO READ ON

More emphasis will be placed on developing a learning culture that has a commitment to learning (Jaccaci, 1989). Growth is now being seen as more than production growth. It is also defined as growth for and with the employee and the organization. It is seen more as an organic activity. This comes at a very fortuitous time. There is an ever increasing need for good mental functioning encompassing both intellectual achievement and emotional competence. As members of the work force become better educated, and more mature, they demand more input into decision making. The learning culture promotes the concept that people can and will expect to work in small problem-solving teams devoted to improving quality and productivity. The organization that rewards its workers for their innovations and creativity is the one that not only will survive in the 1990s and beyond but also will thrive (Gayle, 1990).

Human resource specialists not only will value the well-trained middle-aged worker but will view the employee's ability to perform as a prime necessity. Terminations are a costly alternative to maintaining employees. Heavy investments in employee training and workers less likely to transfer to other locations add a burden to the decision-making process. Human resource specialists are facing personal demands that could impair their employees' performance or impede the organization's progress.

Since both remedial and preventive mental health issues will become an issue during the 1990s, corporations will need to address these areas. As a result, human resource specialists will require skills to provide rehabilitation for those employees who need it. This can be accomplished through a team approach.

Besides the issues the middle-aged employee brings from outside the work environment, other factors impinge as well. Among these are constant changes, information overload, and new computation and literacy requirements. These come as the workplace continues to move toward a global economy. Efficient productivity and sound decision making will be necessary to compete internationally.

The world of work will have to address such issues as training, reward systems, economic security, task design, job responsibility, employee benefit structures, and retirement. The workplace is also changing in regard to more automation and new technology. Each of these issues will need to be addressed in new ways, especially when considering that the majority of the work force will be middle-aged.

Government's Response

The federal government recognizes that it also has a part to play. The U.S. Department of Labor's report "Workforce Quality: A Challenge for the 1990s: Secretary Dole's Agenda for Action" includes a section entitled "Enhancing the Skills of Employed Workers." The two initiatives under this section concern training.

The first, "Research on Training Incentives," addresses the issue of skills training. Research and demonstration projects will be conducted to cover current incentives and how they benefit both the employer and the employee. State programs that provide training through state payroll tax will be evaluated, as well as those industries that provide training vouchers to unemployed workers, and workplace training programs will be put in place through partnerships formed with industry.

Attention will be given to the problem of how to use available workers. Two major projects are proposed: a work-force clearinghouse and additional research on child care. The clearinghouse will provide information and will promote employers who respond most effectively to employees' needs. Some of the areas to be covered under this proposal are flexible benefits, training, and innovative labor-management relations. Research and demonstration projects suggested under the research on child care section of this proposal will look at alternative types of employer-provided child care assistance and how such programs would affect welfare mothers.

Since a major issue for the 1990s and beyond is how to address the impending labor shortage, two other very important aspects will also be addressed. The first will look at employment service reform. In the past, the various governmental employment services have worked out of a labor surplus mode. Changes are necesssary to address the era of labor shortages. It is proposed that a legislative option be developed that would involve business, labor, state leaders, and Congress.

The second part of the endeavor concentrates on the labor shortage. Research is suggested to determine where the shortages are most prevalent. How serious is the problem? Where are the imbalances of labor supply and demand located?

The U.S. Department of Labor (1989) has concluded that although the maturing work force continues to grow, the pool of younger workers will decrease. These demographic projections will have an impact on the nature of work as well as cause major changes in the work force. This, in turn, will have an effect on the needs of society, opportunities for employers, and decisions of workers. Also, demographic and technological changes will influence the industrial and occupational structure of the workplace.

Manufacturing versus Service Orientations

Human resource management has long been guided by tradition. This arose around an urban manufacturing economy that was product oriented. The workplace has been run on a "one best way" of thinking, with workers involved only when the job actually needed to be done.

It is now possible with the new technology to tailor jobs to fit the employee. This means that now, along with this new technology, more training and retraining will be important. A part of the emphasis on training will be the approach used. A 1988 survey conducted by the American Society of Personnel Administration and the Commerce Clearing House for the U.S. Department of Labor (1989) showed that 66 percent of the respondents identified certain types of training techniques to be used. These included self-paced learning, experiential training, on-the-job coaching, application-oriented training, and training in which the workers themselves participate in the design.

Since society has made a shift toward a service-producing economy, many changes are in order. Mid-life workers may find that what was appropriate for them early in mid-life is no longer important or feasible. This, coupled with increased life expectancy and better health until later in life, creates new issues to be addressed. Continuously working until a later age, retiring from the workplace only to want to reenter at a later age, displacement, and early retirement are all part of the new workplace picture.

As a result, employers need to be aware of a wide range of personnel and human resource policies that affect the maturing work force. Positive personnel techniques enable employers to develop necessary employment options to attract, retain, and effectively manage mature workers regardless of sex, race, or age. Jobs and work environments need to be redesigned to meet the criteria that consider physical capabilities and limitations of individual workers. Employers need to consider rehabilitation of disabled workers who experience job-related injuries or illnesses. The continuous education and training of workers are needed to impart new knowledge, develop new skills, and create new job opportunities.

Developing new public policy is an ongoing process, since new issues continue to emerge. Examples include dysfunctional employees, child care, and elder care, to name a few. New management practices are needed that provide greater flexibility for workers without compromising productivity (U.S. Department of Labor, 1989). It is apparent that unless the goals of the organization and the goals of the workers match, neither group's goals will be met. This will be problematic.

Necessary Job Skills

What do middle-aged workers need to meet the demands of today's work force? Current information suggests that middle-aged workers may not have the skills necessary to work within corporations. Their survival depends on the ability of the employer and the employee to respond to the needs of today and tomorrow. To insure that employees are in tune with tomorrow's needs, the American Society for Training and Development undertook a study for the U.S. Department of Labor Employment and Training Administration (Carnevale et al., 1988).

Employee Skills. This study identified the most common skills needed in the workplace. New entry-level workers of all ages, as well as mature workers, will need these skills. Human resource specialists, do your workers have the following list of skills?

The skills have been arranged in categories. The first category is foundation. The particular skill is knowing how to learn. Because of the constant changes that occur within the workplace, learning will be of utmost importance.

The second category is competence. The skills included under competence are reading, writing, and computation. There will be no place for illiterate people of any age.

Communication that includes listening and oral communication is the third category of skills. As the work force moves toward a more team-centered effort, the lowest person on the totem pole as well as the highest needs to be able to listen to others. Each will also need to be able to interact with the other as well.

The fourth category is adaptability, which includes creative thinking and problem solving. This corresponds with the movement toward a greater team effort on the part of all members of the work force. If mid-life workers do not bring these skills from their personal lives to the workplace, they will need to learn them to function at a level acceptable in today's organizations.

Personal management is another category employers designate as necessary for their workers. This includes self-esteem, goal setting/motivation, and personal/career development.

The category of group effectiveness includes interpersonal skills, negotiation, and teamwork. And the final category is entitled influence. The corresponding parts are organization effectiveness and leadership (Carnevale, Gainer, & Meltzer, 1988).

It becomes readily apparent that these categories and their inherent skills are often more advanced than is usually expected of line workers. If the mature work force acquires all of these skillls and implements them, the interactions within the workplace will change dramatically.

Management Skills. Management has also been studied. According to Gayle (1990), economic forecasters and chief executive officers have identified the following management concerns: (1) lack of management foresight, (2) emphasis on short-term gains, (3) failure to incorporate high technology in the workplace, (4) poor federal fiscal policies, (5) lack of coherent industrial policy, (6) low-cost foreign labor and poor use of workers' talents, (7) too little research, (8) too little development, and (9) ineffective public-education institutions.

With major changes in the requirements and skills of both work force and management, human resource specialists will need new skills to effectively manage this changing environment. Simmerly (1990), in keeping with this new challenge, has identified the following areas as essential in developing enhanced leadership skills: (1) dealing with increasing levels of ambiguity, (2) coping with contradictory ideas, (3) managing conflict, (4) creating win-win situations, (5) creating effective marketing strategies, (6) creating and selling visions of what is possible, and (7) integrating individual and organizational needs.

Learning Society

One way organizations are responding is by looking at ways they can provide education and training. The concept of a "learning society" appears to have merit.

The bottom line of most organizations is financial. The question is, "How does an organization continue to be competitive not only in the United States but also on a global level?" Extend this question to include, "with a work force made up mostly of middle-aged workers?" Then add the number of mid-life people with personal problems who are in the work force. It becomes evident that more is being asked of human resource specialists. One innovative response is the development of a learning culture. The learning culture recognizes and attempts to enhance individual employees' learning styles and personality types. It also promotes a greater amount of teamwork, enhanced with a realistic reward system that is broader than money.

Jaccaci (1989), in his article "The Social Architecture of a Learning Culture," contends that businesses need to incorporate learning as a means to meet the present and beyond in organizations. He suggests Jefferson might define social architecture as "the wisdom of the universe revealed in natural order used for the planning and enhancement of human fulfillment" (p. 49). For learning cultures to be accepted and become functional, employees need to be seen to see themselves differently. The learning culture is a vehicle to identify problems of mid-life employees. These problems can then be addressed since a learning culture within an organization is all-encompassing. It will touch every person as well as the organization.

We are not necessarily talking about the problem employee, but the mid-life employee who has problems. These problems may be a result of years of inappropriate behaviors arising from shaming, dysfunctional family systems, addictiveness, or codependency.

Management's Problem

Schaef and Fassel (1988) find that the corporate leaders are going through a rethinking process. The result is a more ruthless, manipulative, and dishonest approach toward employees. Managers can become more rigid, less creative, and less willing to take risks. This is their response to the imperative to change. Ruthlessness, rigidity, and dishonesty are commonly recognized as addictive personality responses. If these behaviors are accepted and condoned by the hierarchy of an organization, then the organization is acting in a dysfunctional manner. The second response is to indicate through words and actions that this type of behavior is normal. Workers who buy into the behavior either already operate in this manner or will have to learn this type of behavior to succeed in the organization.

Addictive Systems

We have just described an addictive system in operation. It is a closed system that presents few options to those involved in roles, behaviors, and thinking (Schaef & Fassel, 1988). The addictive system operates out of a scarcity model, which says there is not enough to go around. It is driven by quantity rather than quality. This is also an illusion of control—an illusion because no one really can control everything. What often happens is that employers and employees working out of an addictive system begin to compromise. They accept that it is all right to cheat, steal, and lie. This is often accompanied with an attitude of "we are okay."

ISSUES HUMAN RESOURCE SPECIALISTS FACE

There are many how-to and self-help books on the market today. They do serve their purpose. But they often do not give sufficient information to the human resource specialist about the reasons or causes for dysfunctional behaviors recognized within the work environment. New and different issues have surfaced that were not discussed in public even a few years ago, that is, codependency, addictions, shaming, good-enough mothering, and dysfunctional family systems. To add to the confusion, some of these labels are misused. The terms have already been so overused that they have been rendered impotent. Once a term becomes a buzzword, it easily becomes an excuse for every behavior. The term then falls into disrepute, losing its value. Yet the behavior itself can be very destructive to the individual and others involved.

Keiffer (1984) recognized that the labor force was growing older. These workers were acknowledged as being more reliable and more ego involved and as having less absenteeism. Illicit drugs were not used, but alcohol was a problem. What a difference six years make! We now know that alcohol is just one of many substance addictions and that there are also process addictions. Both arise from dysfunctional systems and are coping mechanisms. They also affect all parts of people's lives. Addictions and dysfunctional behaviors are major factors regarding employees who have problems that infiltrate and affect the work environment.

These employees bring their problems to the workplace. Their behavior interferes with the employees' ability to interact with each other and with authority. They can become more reactive when major changes are required within the work environment. With the advent of technology, change will continue to be part of the mid-life employee's normal routine.

One response to change is sabotage. More attention is being given to this activity as it occurs more frequently, which, in turn, seems to cause loss of money, productivity, and lives. Sabotage has been around since the 1970s when it was referred to as the "Lordstown Syndrome." The major activities at that time included jammed assembly lines, slashed upholstery, etc. Today, in a technology-dependent workplace, sabotage has been upscaled to include "logic bombs," computer viruses, and database destruction. Sabotage is characterized by a deliberate act of vandalism aimed at damaging an organization. This can affect the organization's reputation, machinery, or operations. Employees who have problems are singled out as the culprits. The question that needs to be addressed is, "Do these employees have problems, or does the workplace cause or intensify the problem?" There seems to be some evidence that both of the above are possibilities that need exploring (Crino & Leap, 1989).

Codependency

A relatively new issue facing human resource specialists is codependency. Mid-life workers can take a good deal of responsibility regarding their work. However, there are those who sabotage these endeavors through their codependent behaviors. Usually these behaviors carry over from their personal lives. Codependency describes people acting out of a particular behavior system or pattern. They always give, never ask or take until the relationships become so impaired that they lash out and everyone begins to act out polar position responses. People begin to overreact rather than respond. All of us are codependent to some degree and may even choose this type of behavior response in a particular time or situation. The question is, to what degree do people act like this and how does it affect others? It is important to recognize the characteristics and know some ways in which to aid in changing that behavior.

Addiction

The "new word" that may soon become obsolete because of improper usage is *addiction*. Addictive behavior is an area that is now recognized as a broader-based set of responses that flow from an addiction. These behaviors may be a result of either substance addictions or process addictions. Substance addictions include mood-altering chemicals that are taken into the body, that is, alcohol, drugs, caffeine, nicotine, salt, sugar, and food. All can lead to a physical or psychological dependence for mood alterations.

Process addictions are a series of activities or interactions on which a mid-life worker becomes dependent for mood alteration. The common process addictions include work, television and/or video games, sex, money, gambling, religion, relationships, and certain kinds of thinking. It is helpful to know that any process can become addictive if it is practiced often and relied on to put a buffer between ourselves and our feelings. All addictions serve to numb us so we don't feel the pain. Subsequently, we don't develop healthy coping skills to deal with the cause of the pain. Substance and process addictions seriously alter our lives.

Shaming

Shaming behavior has been identified by Bradshaw (1988) as one of the major underlying causes of dysfunctional and addictive behavior. The healthy emotion of shame lets us know that we are human. It moves us to seek new information and to learn new things. It serves as a warning signal to correct ourselves, and it makes us redeemable.

On the other hand, toxic shame results when shame is used to control another. It becomes a beacon of our identity, transmitting to ourselves the message that we are defective and flawed. It comes from unreliable and shame-based models. These are usually the adults with whom we came into contact as small children. Since it is from our families that we first learn about ourselves, our future sense of self is dependent to a large extent on how those caregivers view themselves. If they are shame-based, they usually project that same behavior onto their children. The difficulty with shame-based behavior is that it is passed on from generation to generation unless an intervention is introduced to break the cycle.

"Good-Enough" Mothering

If the mother is shame-based, she will not be able to provide "good-enough" mothering. Winnicott (1965) describes good-enough mothering as the ability to provide security to young children. This is important while they are experimenting with separation from the mother as a way of interacting in the world. A small child fears that separation means abandonment. There is the anxiety that outside her presence, mother or self may cease to exist. With good-enough mothering this will be less acute, allowing the child to grow into adulthood with a healthy sense of self. Less than this can cause lifelong fears of abandonment and insecurity.

Dysfunctional Family Systems

Dysfunctional family systems are usually shame-based. One characteristic resulting from dysfunctional family systems is the inability to be intimate. People maintain and achieve nonintimacy through poor communication, circular arguments, games, manipulation, vying for control, withdrawal, blaming, and confusion. The functional role of parents is to model (1) how to be a man or a woman, (2) how to relate to others, (3) how to express emotions, (4) how to fight fairly, (5) how to have boundaries, (6) how to communicate, (7) how to cope and survive, (8) how to be self-disciplined, and (9) how to love self and others. In a dysfunctional family system, parents are not able to take care of the child's needs. In adulthood, the person cannot get enough because it's the child within whose needs are crying to be met.

Work Addiction

Work addiction needs to be addressed as another category. Although accepted as a valued norm, it is quite simply an escape hatch from personal problems. This particular addiction has been described as a killer disease because it destroys relationships and kills people. The work addict dies a slow psychological and physical death. Work addiction is abusive to the addicts themselves and their significant others as well as to the people with whom they work. Often, work addiction occurs as a result of switching addictions. The same dysfunctional behaviors are present in the work addict as in other addictive persons (Robinson, 1989).

What is somewhat alarming is that authors like Schaef warn that we may be living in a society where addiction is the norm. If this is in fact a realistic observation, there is need for proper information, education, and referral to treatment. As a result, fewer and fewer people will become entrenched in addictive behaviors.

HUMAN RESOURCE SPECIALISTS' RESPONSES

Why include all of this in a book on the aging work force? One can always learn and change. Mid-life provides an excellent opportunity. One of the major developmental tasks of this stage of development is to step back and evaluate what has happened in one's life. Another task is to make realistic plans about where to go from here. We are living longer, and it's a good idea to live in a more healthy mode both physically and mentally. Since we will be involved in the work force in some manner for more years than our forefathers, it would be wonderful if it is a positive experience.

Another developmental task of mid-life is to leave a legacy for the generations to come. A healthy holistic approach to life inside and outside the workplace is a valuable legacy. Mentoring also becomes a possibility at this period in our lives. If we are dysfunctional, it becomes more difficult for the middle-aged person to be a mentor.

Trigger events during middle age throw us into a transition, causing us to reevaluate our whole sense of being. These trigger events can range from the death of a parent, a newly discovered health problem, a problem child, a job change, or a divorce. The transitions that accompany and follow these events may look like dysfunctional behavior at its height. In actuality, we experience a normal process of loss, grief, and beginning again. Transitions take time to complete. When the process is finished, we may not look or act like the pretransitional person.

Normal growth throughout a lifetime is not without its pain and trauma. A person changes. This is especially true in a growth process. Part of that process is to become more of what we are able to become. This might not be pleasant for our families, friends, coworkers, and supervisors. They may respond by trying to get us to change back because the known, even if horrible, is preferred to the unknown. Also, one person's change may start a chain reaction. Negative attitudes could surface and be directed toward those who are changing. Now others may be required to change or adjust accordingly.

Human resource specialists need to know the difference between normal change, caused by maturation, and dysfunctional behavior. Knowing how to handle the person who is going through transitions is also necessary. Welcome to the wonderful world of adulthood, where everything changes and nothing changes.

Establishing Your Guideposts

Sometimes it seems that to fulfill one's role as a human resource specialist, one must also have the training and skills of a counseling professional. Having an understanding of normal behavior provides the human resource specialist with a guidepost for determining questionable behaviors. Recognizing the characteristic actions that result from dysfunctional behavior provides you with the chance to clarify what is expected of the employee with problems. It also allows you to make recommendations for appropriate interventions. Knowing and acting on the above won't always be effective for every middle-aged employee. There will be times when termination is the only workable solution. As society becomes more knowledgeable about dysfunctional behaviors, both you and your employees will benefit. Interventions will be more readily available. As a result, fewer mature workers will face termination.

To achieve a better understanding of middle-aged workers, you should know more about dysfunctional behaviors. Since they begin in childhood, let's take a look at some of the reasons why people act as they do.

2

Why People Act as They Do

You are a human resource specialist. Your main objective is to manage employees. You spend a great deal of time either dealing with the employees you oversee or running interference for them. You sometimes wonder what you are really all about. Part of the problem lies in the myth that whatever happens to employees outside the work environment will have no impact on the employee at work.

Throughout the following chapters a number of different issues will be addressed. These will include ways that inadequate or inappropriate parenting causes problems for children, problems that are then carried to adulthood. These are presented for your information. When people know why others act as they do, it becomes easier to identify dysfunctional behavior. Appropriate referrals can be suggested so that mid-life people will have the opportunity to seek the help they need. Sometimes, it comes to either seeking help or losing one's job.

It is also important for you to realize that you are not a counselor. It is not your responsibility to provide any therapy needed by any of your employees. The kinds of problems we are addressing in this book need professional interventions. If your immediate response to an employee's problems is to want to solve them, then you need to examine your own behaviors.

With the aging of the work force, it is important to have an understanding of what normally occurs in middle age. If you will recall, the age parameters for middle age were thirty-five to fifty-five. It is obvious that the thirty-five-year-old is not at all like the fifty-five-year-old. Middle age is a time in the developmental process when people begin to reflect about the first half of their life and make some plans for the second half.

Employees who have healthy self-concepts can experience normal mid-life transitions. However, if you have mid-life employees who have not attended to leftover business from childhood, have not integrated a good sense of self, or are not able to respond as healthy individuals, they may cause you problems.

Until recently, therapists gave only lip service to the events of childhood. We have now again recognized the validity of looking at a person's early years when problems begin to surface. The difference today is that this retreat into childhood serves a different purpose. To understand ourselves today, we need to know where we came from. In fact, that is the only way we can make sense of who we are. In addition, there are behaviors we have internalized that have survived many generations. We are not reptilian. We do not shed our old battered skins and slither away from the problems, worres, and disappointments encountered in childhood. We integrate these issues and responses into our personalities. Reactions to the stresses and situations in our life flow from those coping mechanisms learned early in life. They become our personal responses to our lifetime of experiences. These learned and habitual reactions are brought not only into adulthood but subsequently to our jobs as well (Schaef, 1987).

CHILDHOOD EXPERIENCES

It might not be necessary to comb early childhood for every problem that might have occurred. It is helpful to know that there are some issues that continue to follow us throughout our lives. They do need to be addressed at some point. If behaviors learned in early childhood were inappropriate and never replaced with more positive life-giving behaviors, they can easily intensify until mid-life, when they become destructive to the individual as well as to those with whom the individual interacts.

These inappropriate behaviors usually revolve around basic needs that parents were not able to or did not fulfill. Children need to touch and be touched, to have someone who affirms their emotions, to have structure, and to interact with people who are predictable. They need a trusting relationship in which they can be different but accepted; they need security. Oftentimes food, clothing, shelter, and education are thought to be all that children need. These are important, but there are other needs. There are laws that protect children from physical abuse. In spirit these extend to emotional abuse as well, but this type of abuse is much more difficult to prove. Addressing and responding to children's emotional needs deals with children's ability to respond to the world. Basic needs that are not met through shaming behavior, less than good-enough mothering, and dysfunctional family systems can result in addictive personalities as well as codependency. Adults who are from dysfunctional family systems reflect dysfunctional behavior in their personal lives, in social interactions, and in the workplace.

Healthy versus Unhealthy Behaviors

It is important for you, the human resource specialist, to be able to identify healthy versus unhealthy behavior. In addition, it will be to your advantage to be able to identify characteristics of dysfunctional behavior in order to respond appropriately.

Here is a short scenario for you to contemplate: Mary is a thirty-five-year-old employee who has worked for the organization for five years. During that time Mary has been transferred to three different departments. The major complaint is that when Mary makes a mistake, she is constantly apologizing. In fact, the amount of time she spends doing this far exceeds the severity of the error. Her immediate supervisor and her coworkers lose time and patience with her. When Mary comes to see you, she again apologizes profusely. What would be your course of action at this point?

In talking with Mary, you have reached an agreement with her about the incident, putting it in proper perspective. You silently congratulate yourself. You have succeeded in heading off a potential disaster. As Mary turns to walk out, she pauses and says: "I am so ashamed. I have caused so much trouble. I will never do it again, I promise." If you are listening carefully and really hear the comment she has made, you have a clue. Mary may well be an adult who could never please her parents. When Mary didn't conform to their image of how she should act, she was ashamed. She then tried harder. In fact, she may have found that only after apologizing was she given any positive response. Mary learned early that it wasn't okay to make a mistake. She was shame-based as a child.

Shaming Behavior

One major behavior that seems to underlie most dysfunctional behavior is that of shaming. Basic trust is established through the development of an emotional bonding between child and caretaker. The child learns that there is love, respect, and a sense of caring by the caregiver. It is this sense that allows the child to venture out to experience the world. However, once this trust has been established, the child is able to feel shame. At about eighteen months, the child begins to learn a healthy sense of shame. If the parents are shame-based themselves, the child actually learns toxic shame.

Healthy shame allows us to be human, to recognize that we can and do make mistakes. It lets us know that we have limitations. Caregivers are the ones who expose their children to healthy shame through role modeling with other adults, society, and the children themselves. If caregivers have a healthy sense of shame, then they will pass that on to their children. If children learn to establish boundaries, are able to explore, and can return to an accepting home base, they will continue to grow and mature with a minimum of self-annihilation.

If one of the caretakers is shame-based, then the children will not have a proper role model, will have problems establishing boundaries, and will have a ruptured sense of self. In short, they will perceive themselves as defective and basically flawed.

In fact, toxic shame is so detrimental that a shame-based person is even ashamed to admit feeling shame. It is this type of shame that causes behavioral problems within the person's personal life, social functioning, and work environment.

Internalization of Shame. According to Bradshaw (1988), there are three processes that occur when toxic shame is internalized. The first concerns the caregiver. The child identifies with unreliable and shame-based models. In order for children to know what is normal, they have to experience normal behavior. If the caregivers are shame-based, they will not respond appropriately to situations and events that occur. The caregivers must also be reliable. Here we are talking about consistency as well.

For example, suppose that George, who is three years old, is given a special treat when he goes through a whole day without an "accident." On the other hand, when he wets his pants at any time during the day, he is put in a closet for fifteen minutes. In addition, when his father returns from work that evening and learns that George has had an accident, he tells the boy: "George, you were not a big boy today. You wet your pants. I am disappointed in you." These comments are made with a stern face and a deep, serious tone. They may be accompanied with a threat of what will happen if George wets during the night. The next day, George wets again. Daddy received a raise that day and is on cloud nine. Daddy is told that George wet his pants. He says, "That's okay, George, you are my big boy, aren't you?" Then later in the evening, when Grandma and Grandpa are over to help celebrate Daddy's raise, George wets again. This time Daddy scolds him. Daddy is embarrassed in front of his parents. What will they think of him as a father? Here his son is already three years old and he still wets his pants.

George grows up. He has learned that when something happens that is outside his control, he may be punished. If he is powerful enough, he can control all unforeseeable situations. How will he respond in a work environment? He may be the employee who is never wrong and blames others for every unfortunate situation. Or he may be the employee who is unwilling to try anything new for fear he will not be in control.

The second process involves the trauma of abandonment as well as the perception that it is shameful to have feelings, needs, or drives. Abandonment occurs when children lose a sense of their authentic self.

Roger was born out of wedlock. Though his father and mother never married, his father would occasionally spend time with Roger. Several times, his father left Roger in a park, cafe, or store while the father went to get a drink. Once, Roger's father even forgot him. Roger's mother worked two jobs, so she was not able to look after him properly. Eventually, Roger moved in with relatives. He was in their family but never really became part of their family. Roger ran away. He made up a past that reflected a happy childhood. Roger actually was leading two lives. He kept his real life secret. Sometimes Roger would confuse his real and fictional lives. People with whom he worked wondered whether Roger could distinguish between reality and fiction.

Children who have no model to help them verify feelings, respond to their needs, or help them recognize their normal drives develop toxic shame. There is no mirroring to guide these children's perceptions of appropriate emotional responses. Caretakers are neglecting their children's dependency needs. Children need the parents to be there when they are feeling their way with new experiences. They need to learn that emotions are just that, emotions. There is nothing wrong with experiencing an emotion. In fact, it is healthy. It is by expressing emotions that children learn boundaries and appropriate responses. They learn that parents and children can each have feelings that do not coincide. A parent may be angry, frustrated, disappointed, or sad. A child may also feel any or all of these emotions as well. If parents use any of these emotions to get their needs met, the children will model that behavior. There are parents who give the message that it is fine if they do this, but the children cannot. This causes confusion within the child. In addition, when feelings are not allowed to be expressed in a safe environment, they get pushed down and stored up. Eventually, the feelings come out at inappropriate times and in ways that can be very destructive.

The third aspect of the process of toxic shame lies within the memory. Imprinted in our memory is everything we have seen, felt, heard, or experienced. One of the major problems shame-based people encounter is that the shame they experienced is forgotten. They don't remember being ashamed. This is partly due to their need to survive. They have disassociated themselves from their unpleasant experiences. Here is an example.

Gloria, who is fifty-five years old, holds a responsible position in a large corporation. On occasion, Gloria becomes full of rage over what she perceives as situations designed to undercut her authority. If it weren't for her splendid track record over the years, she would have been terminated following several incidents. Her coworkers complain that Gloria is going through one of her spells again. On closer examination, it is clear that her coworkers also maintain a distance. They do not want to be the object of Gloria's rageful behavior. In addition, several promising employees have moved to other organizations. Gloria is always blaming others for mistakes or errors that occurred. You are asked to review Gloria's behavior. What is your prognosis?

One sign of shame-based behavior is that people blame before they can be blamed. This is a method used to transfer blame. People need to think that the source of the problem is external to protect themselves from being shamed. It would be helpful if you could gather some information about Gloria's early years. This may be difficult for two reasons. Gloria may not know why she responds as she does because she does not remember being shamed. Second, you will probably not be able to obtain the information necessary. As a result, you may have to present Gloria with an ultimatum: either she seek professional help to determine the reasons for her behavior and to gain more appropriate behaviors or she will be placed on probation. If she is actually acting out of a shame-based childhood, Gloria will not be able to adapt her responses without help.

Let us say that Gloria agrees to seek professional help. She needs to be put in touch with someone who understands shame-based children. She will also need time, patience, and support while trying out new behaviors as she mends the damage caused by the traumas she has suffered. It would probably be helpful to provide information to her immediate coworkers. This should include the traumas suffered by children who were shame-based and some insight into the change process. Gloria will then have a chance to recover her sense of self within a safe environment.

It is important to mention that confrontation is not a good process to use with shame-based people because they cannot distinguish between "I made a mistake" and "I am a mistake." They do not have a sense of appropriate guilt. When one experiences normal shame, one can feel remorse as well as relief. A shame-based person translates the experience into another failure for which to be ashamed.

What Are Some Causes of Toxic Shame?

Abandonment. The major cause of toxic shame is abandonment, where the child loses a sense of an authentic self. We think of physical abandonment. This is just one type. Another important element in the child's development is to be touched, talked to, played with. Children can begin to distinguish between normal and abusive behavior. If there is no mirroring to guide the child, a perception of appropriate emotional responses is lacking. Caretakers who neglect their children's dependency needs contribute to the children's feelings of being alone.

Another type of abandonment occurs when children become responsible for their caregiver's needs. This is accomplished either overtly—"If you want mommy to like you, you will . . . "—or covertly, through sounds and looks. Jennie spills her milk. Mommy curses, picks Jennie up off the chair, sets her in the other room, and proceeds very loudly to clean up the milk. Jennie does not receive another cup of milk. She sits in the living room for a time. Jennie learns that she is not allowed to have an accident or make a mistake.

A third way children are abandoned is when their needs are placed second to the needs of the family system. Mickie's father is an alcoholic. Daddy abuses alcohol only at home, but he does so with such frequency that it is impossible for any family member to have a guest in the home. Mickie wants his friends to come over and play. Mommy tells him that it isn't possible because Daddy is ill. Mickie is drawn in to help protect the family secret, which is a family system need.

Children need parents to be there for them as they are experimenting with new experiences, learning appropriate emotional responses, and developing a healthy sense of self. When abandoned, children experience a loss of self.

Toxic shame is passed from generation to generation through shame-based parents who grew up with shame-based parents. Shame-based people seem to attract shame-based people as mates and continue to produce another generation of shame-based children, and so it goes.

Inadequate Role Modeling. Shame-based people cannot or do not know how to (1) relate intimately to another person, (2) acknowledge and express emotions, (3) fight fairly, (4) have physical, emotional, and intellectual boundaries, (5) communicate, (6) cope with and survive life's unending problems, (7) be self-disciplined, and (8) love one's self and another (Bradshaw, 1988).

Shamed-based parents never learned how to interact with others; therefore, they cannot teach their children. They cannot be there to attend to their children's needs. For shame-based parents, children are there to respond to parents' needs.

Shame-based families have rules, as do healthy family systems, but the rules differ. Healthy families teach social skills for appropriate touching and sexuality, proper health care, vocations, maintenance, and money. They also have rules about feelings and interpersonal communication.

A dysfunctional, shamed-based family's rules include control, perfection, blame, and denial. There is the "no talk" rule, the "don't make mistakes" rule, the "don't count on people because they are not reliable" rule. Shame-based children learn that their needs are not important. They lose any sense of their own personal value. They feel that they don't matter. They begin to feel that they don't have the right to depend on anyone. Eventually, they lose sight of having needs and become codependent.

Bradshaw (1988) suggests that shame is the core and fuel of all addiction. He believes that the content of the addiction, whether it be an ingestive addiction or a process addiction, is an attempt at an intimate relationship. Remember, shame-based people don't make mistakes; they believe they are a mistake. One of the ways they try to cope is by dulling the pain through some mood-altering substance or activity.

"GOOD-ENOUGH" MOTHERING

The family of origin is where a child develops a sound self-concept during the first five years of life. How does this come about? The term used in the literature is "good-enough" mothering. According to Viorst (1986), contact with good-enough mothering allows the infant to feel safe both physically and emotionally. Those memories of being cared for become so much a part of us that our actual mother is needed less and less. We can hold on to the sense that we are accepted and acceptable.

Who Is the "Good-Enough" Mother?

The good-enough mother is the one who is there, loves in a physical way, provides continuity, is ready to respond, introduces her baby to the world, and realizes from the start that the baby is a human being in its own right. Then, when it is time, the mother lets go. Good-enough doesn't mean perfect. It means simply that there is enough attention and acceptance to allow the baby a comfort zone from which to grow and to experience life in a healthy manner.

Not-Good-Enough and Too-Good Mothers

On the other hand, too-good mothering can be detrimental. The too-good mother consistently gives too much; she stunts development by not allowing the child to feel frustration and empathizes so quickly that the child cannot distinguish whose feelings are whose. Children need time to form their own responses to the world. If this does not happen, children will then build a wall so that they can protect their core. At this point, they can resist letting anyone know them too well. Parents need to realize that their children will not turn out exactly as they had envisioned. Children will reject those aspects of the parents' dreams that do not fit their wants and needs. Letting go means respecting the children's right to choose and shape their lives. When this happens, the result is healthy family systems or family of origin work done appropriately. When this is not accomplished, then we see dysfunctional family systems.

FAMILY OF ORIGIN

The family of origin plays an important part in shaming, addiction, and good-enough mothering. To achieve perspective, let us look at the concept of family of origin and identify healthy family systems. We will then describe dysfunctional family systems and give some of the more general characteristics of dysfunctional family systems.

Healthy Family Systems

It is within our families that we learn about ourselves. The level of emotional health of the primary caretakers (parents) determines to a large extent how healthy the children will be (Beattie, 1989). The whole family is larger than any single member of that family. The family is a social system with its own set of rules, roles, and needs. If the whole system is in sync, the members tend to be healthier. According to Middelton-Moz and Dwinell (1988) a major deterrent to this is the marriage. When spouses are content and are able to work together, they are more likely to provide a safe, open environment.

This is important, since our core identity comes from the reflections given by our primary caregivers. The chief functions of a family are to provide safety, warmth, and nurturing to each of its members. It provides an environment that helps to establish a sense of worth, an atmosphere in which it is okay to make mistakes, have fun, and get in touch with the spiritual (Friel & Friel, 1988). In a functional family system, roles are chosen and flexible.

Dysfunctional Family Systems

If any member of the family system is dysfunctional, then the whole system is thrown off-balance (Bradshaw, 1988). All families experience such an upset at times, but the situations differ in intensity and duration. The functional family achieves the equilibrium necessary to stabilize itself again. In the dysfunctional family, one crisis seems to occur after another. There may be periods of calm, but very little is needed to set off a major upset. In other families, dysfunctional behavior is always operative. In fact, it is so pervasive that it is almost undetectable to anyone within the system. The necessary bonding is continually being fractured.

Louise asks her mother if she can spend the night with a friend. Her mother tells her to ask her father. When she does, her father becomes irate. He sends Louise back to her mother with a message: "If your mother weren't so irresponsible, she could make that decision. Am I supposed to take care of everything in this household?" Louise goes back to her mother, who has heard the conversation. Her mother tells her she can't spend the night. Louise will have to improve her conduct before she can expect such a privilege.

Louise feels numb at this juncture. She thinks, "How can this be happening to me?" Then, "What can I do to change it?" As the child sorts through her response behaviors, she may find one that has worked for her in the past and use that. Or this event may be different enough that she has no answer. Despair sets in, with extra energy exerted to solve this new problem. Louise could learn that detachment is the only alternative because nothing else works (Middelton-Moz & Dwinell, 1988). Louise is like a lost child who has suffered a trauma with no positive resolution.

Children who have had similar experiences try to recover what they perceive they have lost. This usually includes the warmth and acceptance every child needs to mature in a healthy manner. When they find that they have not been successful, they become angry with themselves. Rage, an outcome of this stage, is directed toward self and toward objects. To keep the rage under control, these traumatized people become involved in caretaking. This is often called the "wounded bird syndrome": One takes magnificent care of others but is unaware of one's own pain.

High levels of denial accompany this behavior. Once people are into the denial stage, it becomes more difficult to convince them that they need to seek help in order to live more effectively. They don't need help for something that hasn't happened. They need to be aware. What seems so obvious to others is totally outside the dysfunctional person's comprehension.

What do these children experience or feel at this point? They become stuck emotionally. There is little chance for growth until a major intervention unlocks the denial and allows these children to get in touch with what actually happened to them. Feelings include emptiness, emotional hunger, restlessness, apathy, anger, detachment, and despair. As adults, these people also question themselves and conclude that they did something to cause these feelings and they deserve whatever happens to them. Taking personal responsibility for all that is negative about themselves and their interactions with others is typical. They have completely "de-selfed." Bradshaw (1988) identifies some of the roles that shame-based children play while growing up.

Roles

Dysfunctional families assign children roles to play. These roles are very rigid and become the glue that holds the family together. Bradshaw (1988) claims there may be hundreds of such roles. Listed below are several of the more common ones.

Scapegoat. Whenever anything goes wrong, the blame is heaped on this child. In fact, this child eventually begins to play the role at the first whisper of an impending disaster.

Hero or Star. Mommy's little boy or Daddy's little girl. These children can do no wrong. If in fact they do deviate and make a mistake, they feel extremely guilty for not living up to the hero or star status. Mommy and Daddy live out their own fantasies through these children. Whenever things start to go wrong in this family system, the hero or star overfunctions to regain the lost equilibrium.

Surrogate Spouse. Daddy doesn't satisfy Mommy's wants and desires, so she resorts to one of her male children. She may even tell the child how Daddy fails her: doesn't pay enough attention to her, doesn't buy her presents, doesn't tell her she is pretty. The child may even learn that sexually Daddy isn't so hot. Dads look to their daughters. As you can guess, being assigned this role can lead to overt or covert sexual abuse by the parent.

Lost Child. Children who are assigned and play this role often sense that they were not wanted. Their best line of defense is to do everything perfectly. They work very hard at being no trouble to the family. They are and continue to be invisible. When the family system is out of kilter, these children try even harder. They are the perfectionists.

Caretaker. These children assume the role of the adult and fulfill their parents' needs. One of the children in the family is very ill. Mother is exhausted from caring for the child. Jimmy wants to help, so he begins to care for Mother. In a healthy family system, Mother would tell Jimmy that he is the child. Children need to be children and do the things that children normally do. If this is done in a loving way, Jimmy can resume his position as a child in the family. If the message comes across in a blaming way, Jimmy will continue to try to be a good boy and do the necessary caretaking. On the other hand, if Mother accepts Jimmy's caretaking from the beginning, he will assume the role of the adult and fulfill that parent's needs while his needs go unmet.

Characteristics of Dysfunctional Family Systems

Authors writing about addictions, dysfunctional family systems, shaming, and codependency identify similar characteristics. Depending on the intensity of or depth of dysfunctional behavior, the following are present: (1) physical, emotional, or sexual abuse, (2) spouses' physical abuse of each other, (3) parents' physical abuse of their children, and (4) other family members' abuse of one another. Physical abuse of children is probably the easiest type of abuse to detect, but detection does not guarantee anything will be done about it. Craig takes a spill on his bicycle in front of Mrs. Jones' house. When he gets up, she notices a huge bruise on his side. When Craig is asked about the bruise, he says that he was hurt playing soccer. The child is very loyal to his parents. He hangs onto them, asking for attention. When he plays with animals, he is very cruel. Mrs. Jones senses that Craig is an abused child, but she does not have tangible proof other than the bruise. Craig, as he grows up, can be either very passive or violent. If Craig and his family do not receive help, this child will exhibit dysfunctional behaviors in his adult life. He may even marry someone who is passive or violent. The syndrome will continue, with their children being treated as they were treated.

Emotional abuse is much more difficult to identify, although the outcome is no less devastating. Craig was probably emotionally abused as well. His constant need to please his parents is a clue. Emotionally abused children do not learn trust. To gain recognition, they often resort to pleasing behavior. As adults, they either seek someone who will continue the emotional abuse or become very controlling of others.

Many books have been written about sexually abused children. These children are emotionally traumatized and may be emotionally dead. They often find it impossible to have any caring relationships. They may repeat the sexual abuse, with people their own age or with those younger than themselves.

Perfectionism. Certain behaviors result from growing up in a dysfunctional family system. Children like Craig may resort to acting perfectly so that they will be accepted by their parents. As they continue this behavior, they may even begin demanding perfection of others. One of the results is the inability to do anything worthwhile. Nothing is ever good enough. The worker who takes forever to complete a task could be exhibiting this behavior pattern.

Rigid Rules, Life-Styles, and Belief Systems. If abuse has occurred, the family usually exhibits rigidity. Certain rules are followed, which dictate interactions within the family system as well as external interactions. On the surface, the family's life-style may be seen as normal. When sexual abuse is uncovered, extended family and friends begin to identify unusual activities and responses. Because family life is private, there is usually no interference from those outside the family structure. Belief systems are also considered very private matters and, thus, inappropriate to question. If this were not so, more situations of sexual abuse could be identified.

The "No Talk" Rule—Keeping the "Family Secrets." Dysfunctional families do not discuss. If Dad is an alcoholic, it is never mentioned. Christopher, who is six years old, asks why Daddy sleeps so much. Mom says that Daddy works hard and needs his rest. On some level, Christopher knows something is awry, but he is not able to verify his suspicion. He is now keeping the family secret. Family secrets are a product not only of the current family system. They are handed down from generation to generation. Learned behaviors continue through the role modeling that takes place within the family structure. In addition, dysfunctional people usually choose other dysfunctional people as mates. If this is an accurate observation, the secrets grow in number and begin to look like a tangled web. Until the people involved recognize that something is wrong, they will continue to behave in a dysfunctional manner. When they seek help, they expose themselves to family pressures not to change.

Kerry's parents have filed for divorce. Kerry's mother encourages her to join a support group for children of divorced parents. Kerry says, "If I join, will I have to tell them you-know what?" Mother asks, "What do you mean?" Kerry says: "You know, Mother. The secret." Mother asks, "What secret?" Kerry responds: "We don't have any money. Dad hasn't been working and we've been pretending."

If the mother is functional, she will assure the child that it is all right. The child then has a chance to break the "no talk" rule. If the mother cannot face the truth, she will probably encourage Kerry not to mention that fact. Or she might change her mind about having Kerry join the group.

Inability to Identify and/or Express Feelings. When children have no way to verify their feelings, they become dead emotionally. They respond to positive and negative events in a similar fashion. These children may learn to pretend that everything is fine. There is no internal mechanism that signals danger. Confusion, pain, and denial become standard behavior.

Triangles. When third parties are called on to intercede, triangles result. Jim and Jane marry. Jim's mother resents losing her son and is unkind and distant when Jane is around. Jim asks Jane to bear with his mother. Jim doesn't confront his mother. Jane doesn't confront her mother-in-law. Jane complains to Jim, who ignores her complaints. This is one triangle. Jane, in order to regain a sense of stability, complains to Jim's sister, Cathy, who takes Jane's side. No one confronts the mother. Nothing is ever solved, and everyone appears to be getting along. Tension is building and is released only through the triangular relationships. This pattern of behavior begins to permeate all aspects of their lives, including the way they respond to their coworkers.

Double Messages/Double Binds. Honesty is absent; denial is high. Everything is going well; you are a bad child. Mommy loves you; go to your room. Children are confused because they can never satisfy their parents. Johnny's Dad tells him to stand up for his rights. But when Johnny comes home with a black eye, his Dad sends him to his room without dinner. Johnny keeps trying to figure out what he can do to get approval and escape punishment. No matter what he does, it isn't right.

Inability to Play, Have Fun, and Be Spontaneous. Children from dysfunctional families spend all of their energy trying to figure out what is expected of them. They disengage. There isn't any time left to play. Fun is not in their repertoire of behaviors. It is difficult to be spontaneous when spontaneity isn't learned or isn't rewarded. Rigid self-contained actions don't ruffle feathers.

High Tolerance for Pain and Inappropriate Behavior. Because dysfunctional behavior deadens emotions, an extreme amount of inappropriate behavior is tolerated. Deep-seated defense mechanisms develop to protect against pain.

Enmeshment. Enmeshed people have difficulty knowing where they end and others begin. Within families, every member is involved in each other's problems. No one has an independent identity. There is an absence of responsibility for one's actions. If mother is depressed, it isn't long before everyone in the family is depressed as well. Emotions run wild and problems are endless. Judy came from a family that was deeply enmeshed. She tries to solve all of her friend's problems. When any of them gets upset, Judy is too. If any gets wildly happy, so is Judy. Judy has no identity of her own. Judy married Herb, who is feeling suffocated. Since he cannot express a feeling without affecting Judy, he becomes more introverted. Judy is confused.

Barbara is the company sponge. She absorbs every feeling and emotion expressed. Everyone counts on Barbara for sympathy and advice. No one counts on Barbara to complete a work assignment. Everyone is her best friend, but in reality, except when they want emotional support, no one spends time with Barbara. For all of her interaction with coworkers, Barbara is a very lonely person.

When most of the above patterns of behavior exist, it is safe to assume that the family system is dysfunctional. If there is any type of abuse within the family, most of the patterns will emerge. Children who are not exposed to an intervention grow up to repeat the behaviors. Since denial is so much a part of the pattern, it takes a major catastrophe before they seek help. Many become codependents.

ADDICTIVE BEHAVIOR

Since there is a direct connection between shame-based people and addictions, it would be to our advantage to define addiction, discuss major addictive processes, and identify clues to recognize addictive behavior.

Addiction is defined as any process over which we are powerless. The process takes control of us, causing us to do and think things that are inconsistent with our personal values. Addictions lead us to become progressively more compulsive and obsessive. Put another way, an addictive behavior is anything we feel impelled to lie about and are willing to give up (Schaef, 1987).

Within an addictive system is the illusion of control: Everyone tries to control everyone else; control is confused with responsibility; responsibility involves accountability and blame. Crisis orientation is a subtle form of control. Addicts and their families learn to live from crisis to crisis. Every event or issue is perceived as a major turning point, with one barely ending and another beginning. Depression is also often used to maintain this illusion of control.

High levels of dishonesty are present because the addictive system is fundamentally dishonest. Addictive persons begin by lying to themselves. As a result, they keep themselves out of touch with their feelings and thoughts. This leads to dishonest relationships and dishonest family systems (Schaef & Fassel, 1988).

Addicts work from a set of belief systems and values that stem from their need to be in control and to cover up. In the second stage of the addictive process, addictive personalities begin to project their belief systems and values on others. They begin to mistrust others, and others mistrust them.

As they are perceived more negatively, addicts find the freedom to act in an irresponsible manner (Nakken, 1988). By this time addicts, as well as those with whom they come in contact, are feeling a great deal of anger and pain. When the stress increases, addicts feel justified in acting out in a negative manner. As the behavior becomes more bizarre, they become more frightened because they then have to admit what they felt all along. They were and are out of control. More time and energy are used to control their lives. Eventually, addictive personalities feel that they are in total control. The paradox is that the more controlled an addict is, the more his or her world whirls out of control. Addicts are very much alone in their own world, longing to be in touch with others but totally unable to do so. It is at this point that an intervention is still possible, but a great deal of turning outward, toward others, is needed to make it work.

Our society makes its own contribution by pushing people toward addiction through its sometimes subtle or sometimes very vocal messages. Look out for number one; live for the outcomes; always be in control.

There are different types of addictions, substance addictions as well as process addictions. They involve the same behaviors and produce similar results. Substances that are ingested alter moods. The major types are alcohol, drugs, nicotine, caffeine, and food. Bradshaw (1988) suggests that the chief reason people ingest mood-altering substances is to deaden pain. The amount of substance abuse is correlated to the amount of pain people feel. Gambling, sex, work, and religion are examples of process addictions. People participate in these processes to deaden pain. Anything that we rely on for its mood-altering capability can become addictive. The key then is, "How much?"

Addictions provide a temporary fix. They also keep people from discovering the reasons why they need this fix. Addictive behavior is further complicated by the controversy over genetics versus environment. Current research findings support the notion that a genetic flaw can occur. Some people have greater potential than others for becoming addicted. This cannot be used as an excuse. Those who are genetically predisposed need to be identified and need to learn what to avoid to keep from becoming addictive. This calls for another type of rehabilitation process. Their pain comes from inappropriate behaviors resulting from their addictions. Those who become addicts as a response to their environment have other issues to address. They need to look at their family of origin.

CODEPENDENCY

According to Friel and Friel (1988), codependency is a dysfunctional pattern of living, one that emerges from our family of origin as well as from our culture. It produces arrested identity development. It is an overreaction to things outside of us and an underreaction to things inside of us. Left untreated, codependency can deteriorate into an addiction (p. 157).

The term *codependency* is becoming obsolete because of overuse, but the concept is very important. There are certain behavioral characteristics of a codependent (Schaef, 1986). Codependents always give, never take. Eventually, their relationships are so damaged that everyone acts out of polarized positions (Beattie, 1989).

How Do Codependents Act?

Codependents tend to react to events and situations rather than respond. They have tunnel vision that keeps them from seeing the larger picture. Codependents worry a great deal. In fact, they find that through worrying, they become important and can control their lives to a greater extent. They exhibit high levels of denial and devalue their feelings. Because of their very low self-esteem, they enhance themselves by responding to and being needed by others.

Codependents take on other people's problems. Since they deny that they have any problems themselves, they make themselves useful by relieving others of their problems. They expect themselves and others to be perfect.

They live compulsively. Do it now; do it right; and get on with it. There is no room for fun and relaxation. They tend to focus on what's wrong. Nothing is ever right or just fine. Someone is always doing something to them, is ungrateful, is more needy; or the world itself is falling apart.

They are unable to function within relationships. Although they seem to be very helpful, thoughtful people, they soon are a drag because no one satisfies them. They are always working to make things different. Codependents also have strong feelings of guilt, pity, and obligation. They are like a coiled spring always ready to snap.

Since most codependents come from dysfunctional families, there are no role models to mirror or to learn normal behavior and responses from. To survive, codependents learn to be passive, feel dead inside, reach out for someone or something to make them feel alive, and give power to other people or things (Nakken, 1988).

ISSUES THAT RESULT FROM DYSFUNCTIONAL BEHAVIORS

Several issues result from shamed-based childhoods, dysfunctional family systems, and codependency. They include the inability to set boundaries, "de-selfing," intimacy, the Casanova syndrome, and jealousy/envy.

Setting Boundaries

Boundary issues result from dysfunctional family systems. The inability to address these issues causes people to have a difficult time defining where they end and other people begin (Beattie, 1989). People's borders are invisible but real. Those who have grown up in healthy families have learned to establish their borders or boundaries. They know how to respect other people's boundaries and know when others are infringing on theirs. Others have grown into adulthood with damaged, scarred, or nonexistent boundaries.

Abuse, Humiliation, or Shame Damages Boundaries. Those who have a high need to control people invade other people's territory as well. They trespass, not aware they are overstepping their bounds (Bradshaw, 1988). When adults learn how to establish their boundaries, they have to remember that they have no ground to give. They can no longer be willing to lose self-esteem to preserve any of their current relationships (Beattie, 1989).

How does this affect human resource specialists? A blurring of boundaries carries over to all aspects of one's life. Mid-life provides another chance for people to learn about boundaries. A major outcome of having poorly established or nonexistent boundaries is "de-selfing."

"De-selfing"

When people do more compromising than is their share, they lose control of their choices, become angry in such a way that no change will occur, and then protect others at the expense of their own growth. "De-selfed" people negotiate their thoughts, wants, beliefs, and ambitions. They store up anger and become vulnerable (Lerner, 1985).

One of the first steps in achieving or defining a self is to move beyond silence and to make clear statements about one's beliefs and positions on important issues. Having become more self-focused, people can then define a responsible position in a relationship, based on their own values, beliefs, and principles. They do not simply react to how the other person chooses to define the relationship. To achieve this, individuals need to lower reactivity and maintain a high degree of emotional separateness from the other (Lerner, 1985).

When people have a low sense of self, they become accommodating; exhibit extreme positions where self is out of balance; cause relationships to become polarized; and reflect supreme competence to cover their problems. When people have a good sense of self, they present a balanced picture of strength and vulnerability; make clear statements of beliefs, values, and priorities; and keep their behavior congruent with these statements. They stay emotionally connected to significant others even when things get intense. They address difficult and painful issues. They take a position on matters important to them while they state their differences and allow others to do the same (Lerner, 1989).

Intimacy

To establish intimate relationships, people must be able to interact with a sense of mutuality and reciprocity. Some people confuse intensity with intimacy. Intensity blocks people from being overwhelmed by feelings or other people. In an intimate relationship, people continue talking. They do not make unusual sacrifices, nor do they betray themselves. Each party expresses strength and vulnerability, weakness and competence, in a balanced way (Lerner, 1989).

The Casanova Syndrome

According to Trachtenberg (1988), some men's compulsion is sex. Why is this behavior discussed? Casanova-type men are not able to develop and maintain intimate relationships. They involve themselves for brief periods of time and then move on. The Casanova who marries continues this behavior. Obviously, this causes problems within the family structure. He may also display this behavior within the workplace. It is helpful for human resource specialists to know about this particular addiction.

These men are addicted to an activity—in this instance, sexual activity. This addiction has been named after Casanova, who was known as the world's greatest lover. To the men who possess this particular addiction, women are the objects of their desire, the source of their sexual pleasure. They use women to validate themselves. This compulsion is not new. As women have gained a deeper sense of self, more economic security, and different life options, they are not as willing to attach themselves to any man. As a result, this particular behavior is being identified more often and more clearly.

Men who live this Casanova syndrome really despise women and their perceived power over males. Researchers suggest this hatred results from the necessary break from the mother in early age. Some men, not able as young boys to move on, remain maternally fixed. As a result, they respond to women they despise. The whole sexual process becomes one of power and control over women.

Jealousy/Envy

Jealousy is a three-person involvement. It is almost always an accompaniment of love. Healthy jealousy continues to prod us to evaluate whether we do love the other person. It also makes us aware that we do not own the other person. But jealousy comes in unhealthy packages as well. Inappropriate jealousy manifests itself in possessiveness, destructiveness, excessive envy. Jealousy in and of itself is not destructive. Envy is a two-person involvement. Envy is the spoiler. It does not allow one to recognize that others can succeed and do well (Friday, 1985).

RECOVERY

When one decides to make any changes in behavior, the individual will experience countermoves and change-back reactions. Others may try to get the person to change back. Meeting intensity with intensity or overreaction serves only to escalate the situation rather than dissipate it (Nakken, 1988). Recovery is a process of reentering the world, establishing new values, being honest, and accepting ourselves. It is also important to remember that processes take time. It is best to move a small fraction and integrate that change before making another small move. Large and dramatic changes often fail.

Recovery Behaviors

Recovery from shaming, dysfunctional, and codependent behavior is a process that takes insight, time, and practice. There are some behavioral guidelines people can use that prove helpful (Beattie, 1989).

Learn to Detach by Setting Our Own Boundaries. This decreases the chances that people can be hurt by others. Remember that one of the results of dysfunctional behavior is that people never learn how to set their own boundaries. They have no sense of intruding on other people's boundaries. The flip side is to learn to deflect those who overstep boundaries. Others intrude on recovering people's boundaries. Sue, until recovery, had a history of giving advice to anyone with whom she interacted. She had no boundaries. During Sue's recovery, many people told her their every sad story, overwhelming her. Sue now needed a strategy to deflect those encroaching on her newfound boundaries.

Establish a Better and More Accurate Perspective on Life. No one is good all the time. This doesn't mean that a person is bad all the time either. Mistakes and errors in judgment are made. Sometimes people are disruptive.

Learn Constructive Problem-Solving Skills That Do Not Include Worrying or Denial. People need to adopt an attitude that they will do the best they can based on the information they have at the time. They then will be able to short-circuit the "worrying" habit. This can be a test of whether they are functioning in a normal range or falling back into their dysfunction. Similarly, people don't have to deny they erred. They don't have to deny their feelings or emotional responses. They can accept and own them and use these experiences as a means to grow.

Jack is a perfectionist, but he is working on deemphasizing this character flaw. A major project is an hour late because Jack misread the deadline time. If he is recovering, he can admit his error and assure that it will not cause ongoing problems. People do accept others when they admit they made a mistake. Denying and shifting problems causes others to become upset.

Learn to Express Feelings. If, as children, we were not supposed to show feelings, then we never learned appropriate responses. It is also possible that our parents expressed feelings but did not think it worthwhile for children to do so. They may have come from family systems where feelings were kept hidden. Several outcomes can result from these rules. Feelings can surface and explode out of proportion to the event or circumstances that caused them. Or, people can begin to disassociate and have no feeling responses at all.

In June's family, feelings were hidden until, as Daddy would say, "That was the straw that broke the camel's back." Then all hell would break loose, and everyone would run for cover. In Jack's family, by contrast, there was no evidence that anyone had any feelings about anything. Most of his family were apathetic or played martyr roles.

Value What We Want and Need. We need to be able to identify what we want and need. Sometimes people turn their wants into needs. Since this is dishonest, there is also a negative feeling about really deserving what we want. Not learning to identify needs in the family makes it difficult to ask for what we need.

Stop Punishing Ourselves for Other People's Problems, Nonsense, and Insanity. When we grow up not learning how to set boundaries and being assigned a particular role in the family system, it is difficult to determine whose problem is whose. We keep getting caught in other people's problems. We interact through the use of triangles. He said that she said, and look what they did to me. If others have problems, approach life in a dysfunctional manner, or act crazy, that has nothing to do with us. We have to be well into recovery to disown these behaviors.

Stop Expecting to Be Perfect and Stop Expecting Perfection from Others. We are told to love our neighbor as ourselves, but so often the hidden message is to be sure to hate ourselves.

Stop Compulsively Taking Care of Other People and Start Taking Care of Ourselves. The only issues we can really address are our own. We can influence only our own behaviors. We cannot control anyone else's behavior. Taking care of others makes them dependent on us. It may make us feel wonderful, at least for the moment, but if the other person becomes superdependent on us, we may feel overwhelmed and used. This type of behavior also robs people of their sense of self, creating dependency needs.

Learn to Be Good to Ourselves, Have Fun, and Enjoy Life. Dysfunctional people do not have fun. They are usually too busy taking care of others. Ethel is serious and intense. She is the one who can be depended on to get a job done. In the office where she works, Ethel is found late at night correcting and cleaning up work done by others. Everybody likes Ethel, but no one socializes with her. She lives a lonely life. She doesn't know how to have a good time.

Learn to Feel Good about What We've Accomplished. Since we were never able to please those more powerful than ourselves, we never trusted our abilities. We worked harder to produce an even better product. Eileen is often complimented about her work, but her responses usually include disclaimers. "It could have been better, but I ran out of time." Or, "I don't know; did you really like it?" In continually putting down her own work, Eileen becomes her own worst enemy.

Stop Focusing on What's Wrong and Notice What's Right. If we are not allowed to make a mistake as children, we tend to concentrate on the negative aspects of everything we do. No one does everything poorly. Most of us do quite well in most of our endeavors. By recognizing the imperfections, we use time and energy that could be better spent enhancing our talents. Success begets success, while failure begets failure.

Learn to Function in Relationships. Relationships are not made in heaven. They take work, dedication, and time. Because dysfunctional people rarely experience healthy relationships, they have no basis from which to judge. Also, dysfunctional people seem to draw the same type of people to them. In recovery, recognize the signs that signal strong, emotionally healthy people.

Learn to Love Ourselves So We Can Better Love Others. We cannot love others unless we love ourselves. We need to be able to accept ourselves as we are. We all have warts and shining halos. When we are able to accept that about ourselves, we are able to accept others. In fact, harping on another's faults is a sure sign that we have fallen off the recovery wagon (Beattie, 1989).

ORGANIZATIONAL INTERVENTIONS

If the organization is interested in keeping its mid-life workers, several interventions can be incorporated. The organization can contribute by providing information, education, retraining, mentors, autonomy and independence, support groups, and when necessary, professional counseling.

Remember Mary's response: "I am so ashamed. I have caused so much trouble. I will never do it again, I promise." Unless Mary recognizes that her response is inappropriate, she will continue this pattern of behavior. If your organization has a program in place, you can help Mary. You can arrange a meeting with a professional counselor. She can attend a support group that addresses her issues. Showing Mary a way to change her behavior is more positive for her and the organization. Investing some time and energy would prove more profitable for Mary and the organization. As a result, the organization would keep an important, loyal, and more productive worker.

George may not be aware that he is a source of irritation and frustration. He uses the survival mechanisms that worked for him as a child and a young adult. Rather than confronting George in order to keep peace, you could stipulate that he seek professional counseling. People like George are usually

very charming. They manipulate people. George always has his loyal following. Although some are upset with him, others think he is wonderful.
These groups change: Not everyone is upset with George at the same time.
When asked, people may even say, "Oh, that's just George." The problem
is that there is always chaos, frustration, and uncertainty. It is important
to stabilize the group. This can be accomplished by helping George to get
in touch with his behavior.

Gloria is full of rage, which has led to less than satisfactory working
conditions. People find it difficult to admit behavior problems when they
are shunned; most of their energy goes into surviving. One of the mechanisms used is defensive behavior. Support groups or continuing education
could provide insights. People like Gloria would have a safe environment
in which to work on their dysfunctional behavior.

Providing reading materials about shaming behavior, dysfunctional families, or addictions to all employees can have a significant impact. Some
people, when given information, recognize their problems. They take it upon
themselves to investigate and to initiate change. The kinds of problems we
have discussed are more serious than the ordinary changes that occur in
mid-life. These problems need major interventions, which require serious
thought, planning, and commitment within the organization. Change is a
process. People who are in recovery try out new and different behaviors.
When support is provided, people complete the process more effectively
and efficiently.

Child to Adult

Dysfunctional children grow up to be dysfunctional adults. They continue
to respond to situations and events using the behaviors they learned on the
way. Dysfunctional families generally produce another generation of dysfunctional families. During the early years of marriage, child rearing, and
work, families often overlook inappropriate behaviors. The world of work
often becomes like a family. If the family of origin is flawed, the behaviors
that result will show up in the work setting.

3

Family Issues as They Relate to the Work Force

Mid-life encompasses about a twenty-year span. Those who are in the early stages have different tasks to accomplish. They are concerned with young families, career goals, and their own sense of who they are. Those in their forties have established their families and are beginning to question job and career. Those in their fifties are launching their families and are seeking job security or thinking about another career. There are exceptions, of course. Women who are starting their families at a later age have different concerns. Displaced workers need to expend their energies differently. Divorce and widowhood force mid-life people to reassess their lives. Restructuring "the dream" is a normal mid-life task.

Regardless of the circumstances, mid-life signifies an opportunity to begin a new life, a new start. People often forget they bring the past along into the present. Unresolved, dormant family issues that have been ignored become significant. Events trigger these unresolved issues. Personal struggles play themselves out within the family and at work.

We have identified childhood traumas resulting from dysfunctional family systems, shame-based families, and addictive behaviors. Patterns that emerge continue to influence people's behavior. Until recently, we saw problem people as weak or inconsiderate. The only addiction identified was alcohol abuse. We recognized the negative affect alcoholism had on family and work, and we focused time and energy on determining whether alcoholism was genetic or a learned behavior. As a result of these investigations, multiple addictions and codependency were identified. After more study, we were able to identify dysfunctional family systems. Now it is clear that shaming is a key to much of the dysfunctional behavior within families and the workplace.

FAMILY ISSUES

Throughout the history of this country, the family was considered to be the cornerstone. This is still an acceptable notion if individual family systems are healthy, but there is evidence that many family systems are dysfunctional. Families can be very violent in nature. Unless these families are identified and appropriate interventions taken, the next generation will continue the same behaviors.

Family issues result from internal belief systems. If parents believe that children have value, they will treat them as valuable. If they believe that children are to be seen and not heard, children are forced to be silent. These belief systems are powerful. They determine attitudes, judgments, perceptions, and behavior, as well as relationships, education, careers, and ethics. In healthy families, parents and children live and grow together. Although mistakes and errors in judgment are made, they are recognized and corrected when possible.

Every family faces unresolved issues that arise from merging two different family systems into one and raising children within this new family. Dormant family issues contribute to the dynamics in the following scenario.

Impact of the Family of Origin

Don and Sue met when Don was twenty-three and Sue was twenty. Don came from a family where everyone talked about everything all the time. Sue's family was more subdued. Now, twenty-five years later, Don and Sue go their separate ways. Kevin, their older child, is outgoing like his father. Mark is quiet like his mother. Don and Kevin spend a good deal of time together. Mark is a loner. Sue blames Don for Mark's quietness. Although Kevin was ticketed for speeding and driving while under the influence, Don continues to support him. Don's typical response is that boys will be boys. Recently, however, Mark was arrested for shoplifting, and Don was furious. How could a child of his embarrass him like that?

Merging Two Family Systems

Investigating Don's and Sue's families of origin could provide insight. Don was rewarded for typical male behavior. The message was, "It's okay to cruise, speed, and drink." In fact, Don's father encouraged this behavior. His mother provided the stability. When Don met Sue, he was impressed. Here was a woman just like his mother. She was quiet, stable, and liked him the way he was.

Sue, on the other hand, came from a family where rules were set down and strictly enforced. Sue was groomed to be the perfect lady. Sue's mother was a closet alcoholic. Her father kept the family together. Sue did not have any close friends because she had to be available at home in case her mother needed her. When Sue met Don, she was attracted to his outgoing fun-filled approach to life. Sue's father was not pleased with her choice.

New Family System

After the marriage, Don became more involved in his career. Sue managed the home and raised the children. In time, Sue resented Don's involvement with work and his preferential treatment of Kevin. Don began to feel trapped by Sue's constant need to have him home. He also resented her taking Mark's side.

Don and Sue's original attraction to each other began to diminish. Although they did merge two family systems, they still acted out of their family of origin behaviors. As a result, they did not create a new family.

Trigger Events

Most people operate on an even keel. They know that some things could be better and some things could be worse. There is no reason for any major change. Then an event occurs that causes something or everything to be questioned. These events, which can happen at any time, cause people to examine options and make changes.

Mid-life is a time when people normally begin to question where they have been and where they are going. Sometimes, people become complacent toward their personal and work lives, and it takes a major turn of events to start this normal questioning process. Illness, death of a family member, divorce, work issues, and children's problems are examples of trigger events. If the marriage is solid, it is much easier to identify and respond to the trigger event. On the other hand, dormant issues can rise to the surface.

It is possible that Don and Sue were content with their family situation until a trigger event occurred. Let's assume that Don did not get a promotion. Mark was arrested for shoplifting. Sue had already begun questioning her purpose in life now that the children were in college.

Any one of the triggers mentioned above can cause a disturbance within a family system. If the system is healthy, coping mechanisms are effective. When these are used, the family functions in a relatively stable manner. In unhealthy systems, any one of the triggers can push the family beyond its limits. Unresolved issues come to the foreground. As the family faces these issues, the effects can extend beyond the home and into the workplace.

Personal Struggles

A family is a unit made up of all the individual members. At times the whole is greater than its parts. Sometimes, each family member is greater than the whole. If individuals within the unit dysfunction, then the family is out of balance. In a healthy family system, there is sufficient reserve to stabilize the unit. But if personal struggles are not addressed and resolved, they become larger than life. Trying to cope with them at this point causes more difficulties. Time and energy are needed to sort out real and imagined problems. It is necessary to determine which problems are a result of this family and which are inherited from the families of origin.

Don and Sue had not addressed their family of origin problems. They incorporated them into their present family system. Don figured that if he ignored situations, they would go away. Sue thought things would get better when the children went away to college. Kevin, like his dad, ignores situations, but Mark is beginning to use negative behavior as his response. Sue feels she has failed in her role as a mother.

Family Rules

How does a family arrive at this point? The members agree to a set of rules. In a healthy family, the rules are discussed, agreed on, and adjusted when they need to be. Rules in unhealthy family systems are usually unspoken. If they are spoken, they are disguised as "shoulds" or "oughts." Because children see their parents as all knowing or all wise, they do not question the rules. As they grow and mature, adult children can and often do begin to question the spoken rules. If the "should" is "you should always put your husband first," the adult woman may question that rule. The problem with unspoken rules is that they become a part of the parents' belief systems. Father rages at or beats Mother when she forgets to buy bread. Mother pouts and ignores Father when he is ten minutes late in the evening. If this is a common occurrence, then children consciously and unconsciously behave accordingly. The boys in the family abuse the girls. The girls manipulate through silence. Unspoken beliefs are difficult to identify because they are subtle. If parents are asked, they will probably deny the rules. What are some of these unspoken rules?

Control. Obedience at all cost. "You will do as I say." "You have no right to question my decisions." "How many times do I have to tell you?" "Go to your room." "You are grounded for a month." Parents become all powerful and controlling. Some children will become model children. They learn to seek their sense of self through ingratiating and pleasing behavior. They never learn to assert themselves. They bury their emotions. Eventually, they respond the same when hurt and when happy. The main purpose in life for these children, as middle-aged adults, is to keep the peace. Their motto is, "Don't rock the boat."

Other children will pretend to be the model child but disguise their true feelings. Some will learn to manipulate to get their way. Others will bury the hurt, rage, and frustration. Kevin is an example of a child who learned to manipulate. As an adult, he will continue to use that response until it no longer works for him. He may then become depressed or become violent. Mark buries his feelings but behaves negatively. He goes to extreme measures to get the attention he needs. He could become harmful to himself, whereas Kevin could become harmful to others.

Conforming. "Do as I say." Learn what is expected and do it. These children do not learn how to make their own decisions. They are followers. Some may not even have the ability to evaluate situations. They just follow the leader. As adults, they can become the scapegoat. They also encourage their own children to conform. The problem is that these children must conform to their parents' belief systems and model their parents' behaviors. Peer pressure and learning outside the home can place a burden on these children. They may reject everything.

Is it bad to be different? Individuality is healthy; it is the process of finding out who we are. Children can then continue to mature into healthy adults. Each person is unique. Part of the maturing process is finding out what makes one person different from others. When people learn this, they can then begin to cultivate that uniqueness. If children are punished whenever they act differently, they learn to be someone else. They lose touch with their inner self. These children eventually become a shell unable to make decisions, respond appropriately, or take responsibility for their actions. As these children grow to and through adulthood, they may continue to act out similar behaviors within their newly formed families and within the workplace. Because of the confusion of forming a new family, responding to children, and dealing with work constraints, the behaviors may not become apparent until mid-life. More is now being written about mid-life people's response to work and their own lives. Some of the information concerns mid-life employees who have problems. These problems may have begun in childhood but were never recognized or were considered too disruptive. As these people began their mid-life transitions, they may have come to recognize behaviors that were not acceptable to them. Others—family, friends, or coworkers—may also have brought certain behaviors to their attention. It is important, as a result, to look at work and family.

Work and Family Interaction

Work and family interactions have increased. There are more conflicts of time and roles within families and the workplace. Working women are part of the change. Although women have always been involved in the work force, more are being employed in professional and managerial positions. A second part of the change is the demise of the nuclear family. Single women with dependent children make up 8 percent of the work force (Nollen, 1989). The third part of the dilemma is the lack of male involvement in typically female roles within the family. Married working women are still responsible for home chores and child care. Healthy family members create support systems to help when stress is high. As a result, they can continue to be productive at work and still handle family matters.

Conflicts between Family and Work

Time is an important commodity. There is little discretionary time and it is the family that is usually shortchanged. Even though most homes have labor-saving appliances, there are tasks that only a human can do. Flexible hours would allow some relief by giving people more control over their time.

Another conflict involves interactive roles. Developing relationships within families is process oriented. The workplace is product oriented. If both parents work, there is the constant need to change from one role to the other. Compassion is needed at home and objectivity at work. When Dad was the major breadwinner, Mother took care of the family. Dad could maintain an air of objectivity both at work and at home because Mom bridged the gap. Dual-career and single-parent families require more effort to move between compassion and objectivity. When roles conflict, stress is present. Either family or work suffers.

Peggy goes to her bank to open a new account. Joyce, the account representative, asks Peggy to wait a minute. She needs to call home and wake up her husband. Peggy waits while Joyce checks in and catches up on the day's schedule. The family-work conflict has now involved another person.

Mothers of "latch-key" children spend a good deal of time on the phone giving permission to or checking up on the children. This can be a mid-life issue. Professional women are having children later in life. Reentry women may conceivably still have teenage children at home. Concentration is split: Neither work nor family gets full attention. This can become stressful.

A supportive corporate structure can do much to lessen the stress and promote increased productivity. If human resource specialists are aware, they can promote policies that encourage employees to make adult decisions. Giving people the opportunity to make choices empowers them. It also reflects trust. If the organization adapts to its employees, chances are good that employees will reciprocate.

When family systems are dysfunctional, family and work both suffer. In spite of employees' dedication to their work, if there are problems within their families, then there are problems at work. Anger, overfunctioning, underfunctioning, and triangulating are behaviors that result from shame-based dysfunctional families. Harmful to the family and possibly destructive within the work environment, these behaviors will be described, along with clues to identify them.

ANGER

Anger as an immediate response is an emotion. It is neither good nor bad; it just is. Human beings who are capable of feelings experience anger. It is healthy and necessary. Anger occurs within a social context. Usually there is some provocation. When Fred is two hours late, Carol becomes angry.

Add some new information. Fred's car broke down ten miles from town, and there was no phone nearby. The situation is now different. When Fred calls to explain, Carol is no longer angry.

Change the scenario. Fred was involved in an auto accident. He is in the hospital and listed in serious condition. Again Carol's feelings of anger are dissipated. She is frightened and concerned about his welfare.

Now look at it another way. Fred is always late. He never has a good reason. When he does arrive, he expects dinner to be ready. If it isn't to his liking, he becomes physically and verbally abusive. Carol may feel angry but may not express it because of Fred's violent reactions.

Tavris (1989) says anger is not a disease with a single cause but is more of a process, a transaction, a way of communicating. Processes are complex. There is no one right response, explanation, involvement, or outcome. Social mores, culture, situations, events, people's makeup, and beliefs are just a few of the variables that enter into the equation.

Healthy Anger

Anger can become a moral emotion that can erode affection, trust, and spirits. Bitterness and revenge diminish the angered person's dignity. The first sign of anger is usually an emotional response. If the anger continues, then it is chosen for a purpose. Lerner (1985) suggests that anger is a signal that hurt has occurred, rights have been violated, needs or wants have not been adequately met, something is not right; possibly we are doing too much for others, or others are not doing enough for us.

This Type of Anger with Pathology

Some people experience anger that results from a type of brain damage. If children suffer physical abuse, they could suffer an injury to the brain. This type of injury might impair their ability to control rage or anger.

Feeling angry signals a problem. Venting anger does not solve it. Anger is something people feel. It exists for a reason and always deserves respect and attention. People do have a right to everything they feel. Cultural norms govern how they express that anger. Some people think that by keeping anger to themselves, they avoid making clear statements about what they think and feel. The more people are nice, the more they will store unconscious anger and rage.

Tavris (1989) dispels this notion. In her study of anger, she did not find supporting evidence for this myth that unless anger is expressed, it is stored. Actually, anger is provoked by something or someone. It is not necessary to respond in a violent manner. The best rule of thumb is to wait until the initial feeling of anger subsides. Then rational means can be employed to address either the event or the person. If rage or hostile responses occur, more than anger is involved.

Responses to Anger

Anger does not occur in a vacuum. Something triggers anger. Anger engenders different responses from different people. Culture, social norms, and family influence people's reactions. There are times when it is appropriate and healthy to feel angry. Betty receives a phone call. When she finishes talking, she slams down the receiver. Her face is red and she is hardly able to speak. She grabs her coat and storms out of the building. Jean receives a phone call. When she finishes, she screams at her coworker about inefficient work habits. In both cases, each of the women has been provoked. This demonstrates two different styles of handling anger. You later learn that Betty's son was stopped for speeding, for the third time that week. Betty left to confront her son. By the time she arrived home, she had cooled down enough to speak rationally to her son. As a result, Betty and her son identified a problem he is having. Betty seeks the help necessary to solve the problem.

Jean continues to act out her anger. Her coworkers stay away. Several days later the matter comes to your attention. Jean is still acting out her anger. You try to talk with her about the situation. She informs you that it is healthy to vent one's anger; it makes her feel better. After some probing, you find that an action by her son provoked her anger. She has taken care of the situation: He is grounded for a month. She also tells you that this child has always been a thorn in her side and that she is going to teach him a lesson he will never forget. His behavior is going to change or else. It is obvious to you that Jean's family situation is out of kilter. Although she identifies herself as angry, her behavior indicates other emotions out of control. This is verified by the chaotic and unstable conditions that surround her in the workplace.

Although Betty was angry she mobilized her resources to seek a solution. Jean feels that aggression is an appropriate response, that continuing to talk about the situation helps to dissipate anger, and that continuing to rage is healthy and beneficial (Tavris, 1989). Jean has bought into some of the myths about anger.

Myths about Anger. There are several myths that have grown up around the use of expressed anger. First, retaliation is a must if anger is to be dissipated. This can be a dangerous move. Remember, retaliation should be directed at the person who caused the anger. Punishment is to be in line with the severity of the offense. If the other person can retaliate in a more severe manner, stand back.

A second flawed notion is that talking out anger gets rid of it. Actually, research has found that talking out anger doesn't reduce but rehearses it. Therefore, ventilating anger does not get rid of it. The anger can become an obsession. People forget the reason but they remember the act forever. Feelings of rage or revenge continue. It isn't anger that is being carried, it is hurt feelings, rage, or revenge.

Problems occur when people get stuck in a pattern of ineffective fighting, complaining, and blaming. This only preserves the status quo. It is far more constructive for people to know their behavior patterns when things don't go their way. Sometimes the best thing people can do when they become angry is nothing at all. Let it go. Most of the time the issue will turn out to be unimportant and quickly forgotten. Keeping quiet gives people time to cool down and decide whether the matter is worth pursuing.

Sharpening Skills

There are several ways one can become better at handling anger. When provoked to anger, learn to identify the true sources of the anger.

Henry is angry when Dave is late with his report. Dave apologizes, but Henry is still angry. Henry and Dave have worked together for some time. Dave feels he can ask Henry why he is still angry. If Henry is in touch with himself, he will be able to recognize and admit the source of his anger.

In this instance, Henry's wife has taken a position in middle management. She comes home late from work, disrupting the family schedule. Henry feels out of control. He wants to be supportive, but he also feels that his needs are not being recognized. Dave suggests that Henry join one of the support groups offered by the company. This doesn't necessarily mean that there will be a happy ending, but it does show that Henry can identify what is really causing his anger. He can use his energy to address the issue.

The outcome could be entirely different. Suppose that when Dave asks Henry what's really bothering him, Henry becomes furious. He then accuses Dave of sticking his nose where it doesn't belong. If Dave has the ability to handle anger, he will call a time-out. On the other hand, if Dave is not in touch with his anger, he may retaliate. Verbal accusations fly. Both men are angry, and neither talks to the other. Their coworkers try to carry on as if nothing happened. The workplace is in chaos again.

Learning effective communication skills is helpful. Someone once said it isn't that we don't know how to communicate but that we try too hard to communicate. If people are not on the same wave length, communication will fail. An example that often occurs in marriages will suffice. The wife says, "If you loved me, you would help me more often." So the husband takes on a couple more of the household chores. The wife says, "If you loved me, you would help me more often." The husband responds: "I am doing more. Didn't you notice?"

The wife had in mind exactly what she wanted the husband to do. The problem was that she didn't tell him. When he did not read her mind, she became angry. Tell the person as directly as possible what it is you want to avoid miscommunicating. That does not mean you will get your way. There are times when the person cannot do what you ask or when the person may not want to. We don't always get what we want, but we can open the door for negotiation if we let the other person know what it is we want.

You must learn to observe and interrupt nonproductive patterns of interaction. Every family can identify a stock list of arguments that are never solved. This is true in the workplace as well. These arguments are a waste of people's time and energy. It is also possible that certain behaviors illicit negative responses. Joe and Ted talk together all the time. They seek each other's advice and share jokes and family news. Carrie, the third member of this team, is never part of the conversation. The only time she becomes important is when either Joe or Ted wants to use her expertise. Carrie knows that it would not benefit her to point this out. Ted and Joe would retaliate. Sometimes the situation provokes Carrie to anger, but she has decided that it is better for her to absent herself for a while until she gains her composure. She then either agrees to cooperate or refuses. There is no bite to her response. Carrie communicates as effectively as possible, negotiates when appropriate, and spends her time and energy on completing her projects. Carrie has learned that to respond in any other way would be detrimental to herself.

There are times when anger is appropriate. The moral use of anger allows people to make choices and to act. Knowing when to act is a key element. Sometimes change requires people with healthy anger to fight against wrongs. Anger is the recognized source of many evils in the world today. People are encouraged to examine their anger. Some find none and are told that they are denying their anger. On closer examination, they do identify rage, hostility, or hatred. If mental health specialists think anger is the cause of all problems, people will receive inappropriate diagnosis and treatment, and the specialists will fail in their attempt to work with their clients. This is true of human resource specialists as well.

FAMILY ISSUES AND THE WORKPLACE

Family issues influence employers and employees. The middle-aged CEO is as capable of being a raving alcoholic as the lowest-paid person in the organization. Rebecca is a very capable and efficient secretary. During her years with the organization, she has been recognized as a master in her profession. Rebecca was recently promoted to the position of administrative assistant to the second vice-president. Although Mr. Williams has the reputation of being a hothead, Rebecca isn't concerned. She has been able to work with all her previous employers. On Rebecca's second day on the job, Mr. Williams returns from lunch to find a phone message from his wife. Fifteen minutes later he summons Rebecca into his office. He is furious with her. He begins screaming obscenities and threatens to have Rebecca demoted if she ever "pulls another stunt like this." Rebecca cowers. She then notices that Mr. Williams is very flushed, and she suddenly recognizes similarities between this man and her husband, who is an alcoholic.

For the first time in her career, she faces a situation that mirrors her home life. Husbands can be viewed as very powerful, but employers who make out the paychecks are more powerful. First, let us talk about Rebecca. She is responsible for her own actions in this situation, actions that will depend on her sense of self-esteem, her habitual responses to similar situations, her view of anger, and the type of support system within the organization.

Rebecca is a codependent. She controls her home situation by pleasing, "de-selfing," and escaping into work. Her level of denial is high. When she leaves for work, she dismisses her husband and family. This allows her to be productive at work. She also takes on a charming demeanor. No one has confronted Rebecca with dysfunctional behavior until now. When Rebecca's husband rages at home, she turns a deaf ear. She leaves, or if she can't leave, she fantasizes about her work and her accomplishments there. She doesn't become angry or stand up for herself. Now Rebecca has a serious problem. The one safe place is no longer safe. Rebecca leaves Mr. Williams' office, takes her things, and finds herself on the street, with no safe place to go. She disassociates, becomes disoriented, and is found wandering the streets late at night.

Suppose Rebecca has a good sense of self. In spite of her alcoholic husband, she knows that what he says and does is his problem. When he rages, she confronts him. He is currently in treatment. When Mr. Williams rages at her, she calmly states that she is going back to her desk. She asks for an appointment later in the day to talk with him. She quietly closes the door and resumes her work. Rebecca is aware that she has done nothing wrong. Mr. Williams' anger was provoked by circumstances outside of her control. She also makes a mental note to investigate the support service available within the organization. If the situation is not resolved later in the afternoon, she also intends to speak to the human resource specialist. These are two different responses to the same situation. We have an employee with family problems interacting with an employer with family problems.

What about Mr. Williams? He is fifty years of age. He started working right after college in an entry-level position and has worked his way to vice-president. He is married and has two children in college and one in high school. Mr. Williams comes from a family where he played star and caretaker roles. His father was a workaholic. He became his mother's friend. Whenever she felt needy or neglected, she called on her son to fix things. Mr. Williams married his high school sweetheart. She kept the home fires burning while he attended college and made his move up in the organization. Last year, his wife enrolled in a degree program at the local college. She is doing excellent work and has been formally recognized with various student awards.

Mr. Williams perceives he has lost control of the family situation. He also recognizes that his dream of becoming company president is not going to happen. For the past six months, he has been depressed. His sense of self has diminished. Polly, his former secretary, began to sympathize with him. He saw her as his surrogate wife. Before long, he acted on his feelings. To maintain a sense of balance within the organization, Polly agreed to leave. Mr. Williams has been spending his lunch hours with her. That day, Polly had told him to either leave his wife or lose her. When he returned to work, there was a phone message from his wife reminding him that she was leaving for a conference that afternoon. He would be responsible for Eddie, the teenager. Mr. Williams became enraged and proceeded to vent his rage on Rebecca. He also discounted her request to meet later in the day. No woman was going to jerk him around anymore.

Whether Rebecca acted in a dysfunctional manner or, as in the second example, joined a support group and made an appointment to see the human resource specialist, you—the specialist—have a problem. His name is Mr. Williams. If the organization is committed to providing services for their employees, you can begin to develop a plan of action. However, if the resources are not available, you find yourself in a predicament. Toss in one more negative. Suppose that the "good old boys" network is alive and well. Men will be men. What happens to Rebecca and Mr. Williams? What happens to the organization itself?

The latter is an example of an organization that is acting in a dysfunctional manner that actually encourages its workers to adopt dysfunctional behaviors as a means of survival. Change will come slowly, if at all. As a human resource specialist, you must respond depending on your career goals, personal philosophy, and ability to work within and around the current structure.

OVERFUNCTIONING

Overfunctioning is a patterned way of managing anxiety that grows out of people's experience within their family of origin (Lerner, 1985). It is not necessarily a result of bad habits or misguided attitudes but comes more from a wish to be helpful or as a response to behavioral patterns of others.

Everyone overfunctions at some time or another. It becomes a problem when employees rely on this process to manage anxiety and stress. Overfunctioners appear to be competent and in control in the workplace. Generally, they do not reveal that they are vulnerable. They may not be aware or they may be too busy taking care of others. They are expected to be strong and to be able to handle any situation. When stress and anxiety intensify, they increase their overfunctioning. At some point they become depleted and may become extremely exhausted or seriously ill.

An employee comes in to discuss a problem. You give him or her several possible solutions. You also tell the person you will intervene. You are overfunctioning. You have taken away the responsibility of the employee to respond. If employees are functioning people, they will thank you for your input. Then they will tell you that they will handle things themselves. On the other hand, if the employees are dysfunctional and used to someone else rescuing them, you buy into their behavior.

How Do Overfunctioners Get This Way?

Overfunctioners play a specific role in their families. They become the rescuer or savior. Others depend on them to right all wrongs. Unless overfunctioners see their behavior as a problem, they will continue to overfunction throughout their lives. They have had years of practice. Change is difficult for people who overfunction. These people bolster themselves by solving everyone else's problems. When someone seems to be at a loss, the overfunctioner moves in, takes over, and rescues. Often overfunctioners do not pay much attention to their own needs, since they have been taught to consider themselves less than worthy of time and attention. Overfunctioners are prone to burnout and don't know it is happening or why. Their response is: "Let me help you. You have so much to do; you are not feeling well; you are not so smart." They gain their purpose in life by aiding someone else (Lerner, 1989). Those who were given the caretaker role in a dysfunctional family often grow up to be overfunctioners. This is the only response they know.

An Overfunctioning Person in the Work Force

You have received three different complaints about Claire. Her fellow workers label her a nosy, intruding person. She has taken full responsibility for the success and the failure of the department. When Emily, the secretary, had a problem with her child, Claire covered for her and learned about sensitive family matters. Now that Emily has things under control again, Claire continues to ask her questions about the child and other personal matters. Claire also never fails to remind Emily that Claire helped her out. If Emily is having a bad day, Claire tells everyone how they should respond to Emily. She tells them about Emily's problems. Claire justifies her behavior by telling everyone she knows what is best for Emily. After all, she knows Emily better than everyone else.

Claire overheard Harry, her employer, say that he forgot his wife's birthday. Claire thus has appointed herself his personal memory bank. She reminds him of birthdays, anniversaries, and meetings. Though Harry appreciates some of the reminders, the constant intrusion is beginning to wear on him. Her response to Harry's complaint is that he doesn't appreciate all the time and energy she spent to make him a prompt, efficient employer and a sensitive husband.

Claire's associate, Tom, is an underfunctioner. Whenever Tom has a problem, he goes to Claire. Tom cannot sign off on a project without getting Claire's approval. As a result, he often misses deadlines. The rest of the staff either confronts him or remains silent. When Claire steps in and rescues Tom, others resent her involvement. They want Tom to take responsibility for his own actions. The department is in chaos.

Claire's own family life is totally out of control. She has very little time or energy to deal with even mundane situations. She expends herself totally in the workplace. Her children are constantly calling her to gain support and recognition. Her husband needs to check in every time they have a social or family engagement. Between taking charge of everyone's problems at work and answering her family's calls, Claire does not have time for her work, which is usually late, unfinished, or of poor quality.

Difficulties Overfunctioners Face

Overfunctioners do not deal with their own issues. They appear to have everything together. They never need help, but they are always the first person available whenever there is a crisis. They get their sense of self from being there for others. No one can continue to operate on this level for very long. Soon overfunctioners begin to feel resentment. The early rewards disappear. People become dependent on them, begin to take advantage of them, and give no thought of taking without giving anything in return. Overfunctioners start to feel that they are carrying the world on their shoulders. Resentment and hostility replace their usually cheerful responses.

What do you need to know to give insight and guidance to the overfunctioner? It is emotionally painful for people with this type of dysfunctional behavior to change. They do not admit their own vulnerability and can become anxious, hostile, and resentful. They did everything they were supposed to do and do not know why they feel so badly. Not only do they feel badly, but now they are told that their behavior is dysfunctional. They need to learn to get in touch with their own feelings and to talk about them. They need to accept that it is all right not to be perfect, be always in control, have all the answers.

Claire probably needs more help than you are able to give her. You can start the process, though. You can point out the situation as it exists in her department, share some of the complaints, and direct her to support groups that deal with her particular behavior.

Overfunctioners use distancing when the stress level is too high. There are times when moving away from a particular problem or person is healthy. The distance gives space and time, and all parties involved have an opportunity to gain a different perspective. But overfunctioners cannot handle distancing by others. They feel they have lost control of the situation. Overfunctioners use distancing to lessen stress and anxiety and to deny that they have any part in the problem.

Take Claire, for instance. After your talk with her, Claire may become hostile and frustrated. The hostility comes from her inability to recognize other people's boundaries. She does not have a clear sense of her own boundaries and does not know when she is intruding on others. She responds heatedly: "After all I've done for her, him, or them. You won't catch me helping anyone again." She will probably storm out of the room, pout, and refuse to speak with others. Sometimes, it appears to make more sense not to confront people like Claire for the good of the whole. Equilibrium is damaged when she interferes and when she decides to distance.

Because humans are social animals, Claire either will stop distancing or will change jobs. If she is allowed to continue overfunctioning, the workplace will continue to experience chaos. Encouraging Claire to change her behavior with organizational support will lead to a healthier, happier work environment. While the change is taking place, there may be some tense moments. Claire and her coworkers may have feelings of frustration, and Claire may experience confusion. She acted out of her life pattern of behavior. She has spent so much of her time and energy in making things work and now people are telling her it is inappropriate. Reminding people like Claire that they need to take care of their own issues is an important step. Overfunctioners need to be reminded that the only behavior they can affect is their own. As Claire begins to change her behavior at work, she can also begin to control her home situation.

Everyone who overfunctions needs an underfunctioner. Everyone underfunctions at times in response to a situation or person. It becomes a problem when people choose to operate this way most of the time. Whereas overfunctioners are usually the oldest or only child, underfunctioners are usually the youngest child.

UNDERFUNCTIONING

Underfunctioners have difficulty when they are anxious or stressed. They become less competent. This behavior is reinforced, since there is usually an overfunctioner waiting in the wings to take over and rescue. The role the underfunctioner plays in the family often revolves around, "What are we going to do about this child?" The underfunctioner allows the family to focus on pseudoproblems rather than real problems. Children learn that underfunctioning makes a contribution to the family. They become the focus of attention, which lessens stress and anxiety. As a result, they become the "needy child," the "always in trouble child," or the "child who needs to be rescued." They never look capable or strong. They too suffer (Lerner, 1989).

Why do these behaviors occur? In a dysfunctional family system, direct communication with and between members is absent or confusing. Because of mixed messages, confrontation is impossible. As a result, acting out inappropriate behavior refocuses the problem. Stress and anxiety are ever present. People who have not learned healthier behaviors by mid-life may find themselves forced to reevaluate their behavior. If this does not occur within the family structure, chances are these behaviors will become apparent within the work setting.

One of the ways people choose to counter stress and anxiety is by involving others. Another way is to blame others. Both of these can result in triangles.

TRIANGLES

Triangles are one of the outcomes resulting from dysfunctional behavior and ineffective indirect communication. Their major function is to take the pressure off when issues become too hot (Lerner, 1989). Everyone becomes involved in triangles at some time or other. What are they? What causes them? Why do people use them? What can you do when they intrude into the workplace?

Description of Triangles

A description of triangles is thinking in threes. Gossip is an example of triangulating. Gossiping is a way of life for some people. The level and the intensity of the gossip are the key. If people constantly choose this form of communication, they may be insecure. To feel better about themselves, they gossip about the shortcomings of others. If they are experiencing a good deal of anxiety about their own lives, they may refocus by diverting the attention to others. Harmless gossip includes passing on information. Gossip becomes troublesome when it is used to reveal other people's perceived incompetencies. Whenever a triangle operates, a third person is brought into the question.

Kinds of Triangles

Triangles take on countless forms. When tensions rise between two parties, a third party is included. This tends to reduce or deflect the anxiety. Issues from one relationship or situation emerge and fuel the fire.

Eternal Triangle. This is the most recognized form of triangle. The marriage is faltering. One or both of the spouses seek an outside person to diffuse the intensity of the situation. The third party bolsters one of the spouses' sense of self. When that spouse has achieved enough distance and regained a better perspective, the spouse can then reengage in the marriage.

Ruth and Frank have been married for twenty-five years. They silently agreed that Ruth would raise the children and Frank would support them. Now that the youngest child is almost self-sufficient, Ruth is reevaluating her life. Her role as mother is finished. She has suggested several times that she would like to finish her degree and begin a career outside the home. Frank is involved in a major two-year project. He works sixty to seventy hours a week. He has a supportive team whose members have become close. Whenever Ruth brings up the subject of changing her focus, Frank is silent. He is afraid he will lose his wife's support if she begins to focus on outside activities.

Frank starts sharing his concerns with Maude, a member of his team. She is responsive to his concerns. Over time Frank sees Maude as his confidant, friend, and emotional support system. In the meantime, Ruth goes ahead with her plans. There is little communication at home. Frank spends more of his leisure time with Maude. The result is the eternal triangle. Maude turns down a transfer and starts asking for more support from Frank.

Ruth graduates and begins to build a career as a consultant, working out of an office in their home. In time, Ruth notices how little Frank is at home. When she addresses this issue, Frank becomes angry. He accuses her of abandoning him when he needed her support.

Suppose Ruth discovers that Frank is involved with another woman. Ruth gives Frank an ultimatum: Either he break off the affair or she will leave him. There are several possible scenarios. Frank breaks off the affair, Ruth and Frank work out their problems, and the eternal triangle has served its purpose. It carried the couple through the rough times. Or, Frank refuses to break off the affair but decides to pretend he has. Ruth trusts him. Six months later, Ruth discovers that Frank didn't carry out his end of the bargain, and she sues him for divorce. Frank had never had any intention of leaving his wife and family. He had simply wanted someone to be there for him when family issues became too intense. A third possibility is that either Frank or Ruth decides to end the marriage when the affair surfaces the first time.

Children as Potential Triangles. When personal or family issues become too intense, children are often used to diffuse the anxiety. They become the focus of attention. When the stress between Connie's parents becomes too intense, she reacts. Recently Connie was arrested for possession of a controlled substance. Her parents refocused on Connie's problem, and Connie became the center of attention. Her parents forgot their problems for the moment. Connie was playing her role. Jennifer, her older sister, overfunctions whenever Connie gets into trouble. She maintains the household so the parents are free to worry about Connie. She also is called on for advice: "How do we handle your sister?" Jennifer is pulled into the problem. The parents alternate between children to form a triangle. Each of the girls depends on one of the parents to create another triangle. No problems are solved. The covert anxiety and tension are masked.

Therapists as the Third Leg of a Triangle. Most people expect that therapists are completely neutral. There are occasions, however, when therapists become involved in triangles. Anytime therapists take sides with one of the members of a family, they become part of the problem (Scarf, 1987).

Causes of Triangles

Family secrets are the major cause of triangles. Almost every family has its secrets. Dysfunctional families have more than their share. One of the reasons they are dysfunctional are the secrets. It takes time and energy to preserve a secret; major secrets are forgotten or denied. The latter happens when people who keep the secrets disassociate from their internal self.

When the family members keep a secret from others, certain behaviors occur in that family's interaction. Although others may not know what the secret is, the behavior is off kilter enough that they know something is not right.

Lynn's mother was pregnant with her before she married. Lynn often wondered why her mother mistreated her. The family did not maintain extended family ties, and no one talked about the early years of the marriage. In her middle years, Lynn learned the secret, which the family still maintains. Anytime Lynn encounters anything that can be perceived as secretive, she reacts. The initial, basic trust important to children was never established. Even though Lynn is aware of the cause of her reactive behavior, she still overreacts in perceived secretive situations. This behavior is troublesome in relationships and at the workplace. Friel and Friel (1988) found this type of behavior and response to be common in dysfunctional families.

Responses to Triangles

To understand triangles, one needs to know what unresolved and unaddressed issues from early childhood are being played out. Then it is important to question what the person's part is in maintaining the triangle.

Remember that triangles involve three people who interact to lessen anxiety or tension for one of the members of the triangle. It is difficult to identify early childhood issues in a work setting.

Secrets. People who form triangles often have difficulty distinguishing between privacy and secrecy. All people have a right to their privacy. Some people are more private than others. People who come from dysfunctional families react to privacy, mistaking it for secrecy. They come from families in which secrets were the norm. In many cases, they were the victims of these secrets. They may need help in distinguishing when something is private and when it is a secret.

Dos and Don'ts about Triangles. When you meet people who use triangles, encourage them to deal with the person with whom they have a problem. They must deal with conflicts directly. Second, point out to them when they use others as a go-between. This includes using you, as well. The best place to deal with the problem is where it originates. If the problem cannot be solved, then bring it to someone else's attention.

There are some clues that can aid the human resource specialist in determining whether childhood issues are involved. One is the amount and depth of anger the person creating the triangle exhibits. If the response is greater than called for by the event or person causing the anger, the person is overreacting. This is a behavior you can question. If you can proceed in a calm, dignified manner, you may get the person to identify certain aspects of the situation.

There are at least two possible outcomes. First, the person may recognize that the events triggered something from the past. This dissipates the anger toward the situation or person. People can save face by owning responsibility for their own actions. With a little encouragement, they can seek the person who caused the anger. Most of the time, this direct communication will solve that particular problem. But another problem still exists. The overreactor who identified the trigger needs to talk with a professional to get help. If this does not occur, the person will continue to overreact each time a similar trigger situation occurs. If the overreactor refuses to seek help, you will need to set up some guidelines. If you have auxiliary support systems in place, this task will be easier. If you do not, then you will have to work within the structure available to you.

Second, the person may blame someone or something else. This is a strong clue that you are faced with a bigger problem. Even if you are able to dissipate the anger of this particular incident, the person will likely continue to involve others in triangles. Someone—never the same person—will always be on the "outs" with the overreactor. This will undermine trust and honesty and will damage productivity.

Events that trigger childhood issues will continue to happen, but the person will find it difficult if not impossible to acknowledge this reality. Because every organization is set up differently, it is difficult to give specific recommendations on handling this employee. You need to be direct and straightforward with the employee, set some parameters, and follow through. Otherwise, you will be continually putting out brushfires.

These people develop triangles to handle situations. There are also those people who readily become a part of the triangles. If you have workers who always seem to be in the heat of things, you need to ask them why they always participate. You will probably find that they are codependents or overfunctioners who need this kind of involvement. It enhances their sense of self and gives them a sense of importance. These people also need an intervention. Triangles take time and energy away from the job. They tend to lower productivity and take a toll on motivation.

Sometimes the triangles occur because of a home situation. Although employees can become involved, it isn't a work force issue. The results are the same, however. The triangle drains time and energy needed on the job. Productivity again can suffer.

Whenever people change behaviors, there is always a chance that someone will try to sabotage their efforts. Changes in behavior brought about because of work force interventions will cause changes at home as well. Employees will continue to need your support and assistance to make the necessary changes.

When one person changes, all are affected by that change. It is important to realize that even if employees want to change, they face other employees who do not want them to change. It may become necessary to work with the other employees on the change process. Have materials handy. The other employees can read and gain a better understanding about the change process.

Employees with problems also face their families, who may not wish them to change. You might ask a family to come in and attend support meetings. A second way to handle this could be to have materials available for employees to give family members.

There is growing evidence that the relationship between work and home lives is more pronounced than once thought. In fact, it is essential to address this interaction to make the workplace as functional as possible. If the problems are intense, then outside counseling may become necessary. Most family counselors encourage all members of the family to meet and discuss issues, interventions, and recovery. Employees and supervisors who work with employees who have problems could also attend these meetings. Your encouragement and support are essential if the intervention and recovery are to work.

SEXUAL ADDICTIONS

Another major dysfunctional behavior that affects family and work is that of people who are addicted to sex. Sexual harassment within the family, society, and the work force is gaining more attention. Some women use their sexuality to achieve their goals. But because men have held the power and have been in control longer, they more frequently abuse their relationships with women. The Casanova (Trachtenberg, 1988) habitually seduces and abandons women. He does so because he has a negative sense of self and sees women as a means of increasing his sense of self.

Common Traits

Although Casanova men vary in the ways they use their addiction, they seem to possess certain common traits. First, they are strongly drawn to women. If they are not involved with a woman, they suffer from depression and anxiety. Their lives are organized around pursuing and conquering women. When they fail at this task, their lives collapse.

They are not able to form strong attachments to any one woman. Even after an intense or long-lived involvement, there is little grief, and this grief ends as soon as they find another woman. When they are involved in longer relationships, they are habitually unfaithful.

They begin their relationship quickly, moving rapidly to fulfill their sexual urges. They are not interested in courtship and are unwilling to postpone gratification. They are artful seducers. If they are rejected, they lose interest.

They impulsively fall in love. Their affairs usually end as abruptly as begun. Although they enjoy sex, they measure satisfaction in quantitative terms. Their sexual desire, unlike that of most men, does not grow out of intimacy. They are attracted to strangers.

Casanovas are habitual deceivers. They assume different identities when they are pursuing a particular woman. They see love as a set of demands and obligations. They avoid women who show signs of loving them. They use money as an attraction. Wining and dining women and buying them expensive gifts are part of the seduction process.

As in all addictions, frequency and intensity separate the occasional behavior from the addictive behavior.

HUMAN RESOURCE SPECIALISTS' RESPONSES TO DYSFUNCTIONAL BEHAVIORS

Although what you can do regarding dysfunctional behaviors that result from childhood experiences is limited, it is important that you recognize clues and symptoms. If part of your responsibility is to respond to complaints about workers' behaviors or their productivity, it is helpful for you to know a little about why people act as they do. Simply warning people about their behavior does little to change that behavior. This is especially true for people who are still behaving as they did when they were children.

If you are able to recognize certain types of behaviors, you will be more able to talk with the individual. You can also be more effective in suggesting alternative behaviors or places these mid-life workers can go for additional help.

The workplace can reinforce certain addictive behaviors. If a large percentage of the work force has some type of addiction, those workers who do not could begin to act in a similar fashion in order to survive. If the organization is dysfunctional because those who make the major decisions are dysfunctional, you have a more difficult problem with which to deal.

Rather than present you with a handy check-off list, or a cookbook of dos and don'ts, I strongly suggest that you read some of the current literature on dysfunctional behavior within the workplace. It would be helpful to talk with service providers who deal with this type of behavior. Check-off lists and recipes for successfully altering behavior can be more dangerous than helpful. One of the major negative factors is that after the check-off list has been used and the recipes followed, some people will not have changed at all. This can lead to an even greater sense of failure. Since each person and situation is unique, these methods prove to be too simplistic.

4

Mid-Life, a Time of Change

Defining mid-life is not any easy task. The term suggests that it is the middle of life. Men today have a potential of living to be about seventy-eight years of age. The average life span for women is about eighty-four years of age. This would make thirty-nine about the middle of a man's life whereas forty-four would be the middle of a woman's life.

The term, the middle years, is also found in the literature. This is the time after early adulthood until a person is considered old. Neugarten (1968) says that a person is old at about seventy-five years of age. Obviously, people are not considered middle-aged until later in life. It is difficult to imagine that people who are age fifty-five to sixty fit the description of older adults. They also do not fit our commonly accepted sense of middle-aged. Society incorporates them into the middle-aged group but also treats them as a special group. Since chronological age falls short of identifying how "old" people are, it is helpful to look at the roles people play.

People no longer fit neat packages. Women are having children at a much later age. Fathers are also older. People are living much longer. Men and women are moving from their major work role at a much earlier age. It is not uncommon for middle-aged men and women to begin a new family during these years.

Identifying the issues mid-life people need to address provides an effective place to start. These issues begin to emerge around age thirty-five and continue until about age fifty-five. It is important to realize that these ages are merely a chronological guide. The issues and tasks within these age constraints are more similar. That is not to say that people younger than thirty-five and older than fifty-five may not also be addressing the same issues.

There are several proposed theories of mid-life. By becoming familiar with these, human resource specialists can begin to understand the scope of change that occurs during this period in the life span. Like other developmental periods, mid-life poses particular tasks to complete. When these tasks are addressed, people can move to the next stage of life more easily and gracefully. One of the major tasks of this period is to recognize and respond to the losses that seem to be part of mid-life. One of the major ways individuals can respond to the tasks and losses is through the process of transitions. At times, the changes that occur may stress individuals. They may find that their normal approach to change is insufficient to meet these challenges. Organizations can help through the use of employee assistance programs (EAPs).

THEORIES OF MID-LIFE

Developmental Theory

The first theory is the developmental theory, which has several major characteristics. The first characteristic focuses on the individual and emphasizes personality, as well as social and cultural factors. The psyche plays an important part in this model. A second characteristic notes that the impetus for change lies within the individual. Third, developmental change is observable. In this model a failure to complete a developmental task at any life stage undermines the ability to respond to future stages effectively.

Different Approaches to Developmental Theory

Some theorists link development to specific chronological ages that identify specific developmental tasks. They also recognize elements of continuity versus discontinuity. Levinson's work (1978) is an example of developmental periods linked to specific intervals. These include the patterning of events, relationships, achievements, failures, and aspirations in a person's life. He suggests that understanding the life cycle as a journey from death to life enhances people's understanding of their lives. There is a universal pattern that follows a basic sequence. Within this pattern is a series of periods or stages joined by bridges, which Levinson calls transitions. They can be translated into the time during which the process is in operation. Transitions do not occur overnight. They can take several years to complete.

The mid-life transition is important. Jung (1933) recognized this when he suggested that the purpose of the first half of life is entirely different from that of the second half of life. One of the major tasks of mid-life is to learn more about the internal workings of the person. Although others have discussed this process, Levinson's four polarities provide a clear road map. He defined four: young/old, destruction/creation, masculine/feminine, and attachment/separation.

Young/Old. Although people still see themselves as young, they also recognize that they are growing older. Coming to terms with this allows people to continue to reevaluate those thoughts and actions that worked for them. They also alter or change whatever needs to be changed so that they can continue on their life's journey.

Max looks in the mirror one morning. He sees bags under his eyes, graying hair, and a slight bulge around his midriff. He could very appropriately ask himself, "When did this happen?" Suddenly he realizes that externally he no longer looks like the person he remembers seeing in the mirror. He has at least two options. He can dye his hair, have a face-lift, start exercising, and change his style of dress. If he chooses this option, he will likely make other changes in his life as well, changes directed toward helping him regain his youthful appearance. He may continue on this path only to realize in time that the path is a dead end. Or he can continue to seek his youth. The former is a normal response. If he chooses the latter, he could become stuck.

Cynthia has the same experience. One day she sees this middle-aged woman staring back at her. She too can make a choice. She can alter her hair style, makeup, and clothing. She may even decide she wants to change her life-style. Perhaps she decides that she wants to be a cocktail waitress or that she no longer wants the responsibility of a family. If Cynthia chooses this route, she too could become stuck. But if Cynthia realizes that she is entering the second half of life, she could decide to make other dramatic changes. She could become involved in different activities as well as change her exterior image.

Destruction/Creation. This polarity brings into focus people's sense of mortality. They recognize the destructiveness they have perpetrated. They also notice other people's destructive behavior and the impact it had on them. Forgiveness is the key. People forgive others for the unintentional as well as intentional hurts that have accumulated. They accept that others either intentionally or accidentally can be destructive. If mid-life people cannot let go and move on, they harbor resentment. In the end, they sabotage their own growth. No one can completely rid himself or herself of the potential for destruction, but people can begin to recognize and act on their ability to create. If they concentrate on this, then mid-life can become an exciting and challenging period.

Max, after years of pursuing his youth, realizes that he is losing his wife and family. When they confront him about his egocentric life-style, he becomes angry and resentful. He creates an even larger chasm. He wants what he wants when he wants it. No one is going to stand in his way. He leaves his wife and alienates his children. In his mind, Max is convinced that the problem is theirs and not his.

Max did have a second option available. He could have come to terms with his need to pursue youth. He could have recognized that he was causing pain to others. Through this recognition of inappropriate behavior, Max could have chosen to create a healthy, happy approach to life.

Masculine/Feminine. Male and female refer to gender. Society provides powerful messages about appropriate roles for men and for women. Men select and adopt the gender images they wish to incorporate into their life. In the past, women probably did not specifically choose as much as respond to society's message. Women are gentle, caring, and smart, but not too smart. Men are tough, powerful, and in charge. Gender in most societies defines men as masculine and women as feminine. But this separation is beginning to break down. Younger men are choosing to be the caregivers, the nurturing ones. Women are pursuing more traditionally masculine endeavors.

Mid-life people today encounter more traditional attitudes toward the roles of men and women. Femininity in men traditionally has led to questions about homosexuality. Although there is little correlation, this taboo does interfere with men's ability to identify and live their more feminine side. Mid-life women face similar problems. They were not encouraged to pursue life-styles or careers that crossed over to typical male pursuits. Women were expected to provide a proper home for the men and for their children. If women worked outside the home, they were nurses or teacher.

Power is another issue. Men are powerful. They control. Women are weak, submissive, unassertive. People who are in mid-life today grew up in a time when these stereotypes were predominant. As these people move through mid-life, they meet this issue. If they come to terms with the struggle and allow their opposite side to grow, they will find their lives enriched.

Attachment/Separation. Men and women approach life differently. Men choose to separate from others; they prefer not to become too close. Women are more likely to want to feel part of another's life. This, according to Rubin (1983), begins in early childhood. Boys are subtly encouraged to separate from their mothers. Mother knows that her sons are not like her. They need a male influence from which to learn appropriate male responses. Mother recognizes that her daughters are like her, and daughters are not encouraged to separate. At some point, daughters need to break away from their mother. This is difficult because mothers and daughters are more alike than different. Young women need to learn to interact with a man; thus, their interactions include three people. Young boys, interacting with the male role model in their lives, continue to operate in a dualistic manner.

Problems do occur for males and females. Males can experience problems because the break from the mother comes before they are able to understand what is happening. This could lead to some feelings of distrust, at least subconsciously, of other women. Will these women also leave me? They resist giving themselves over completely to another woman. The wife says: "My husband doesn't talk. I don't know what's going on." The husband is confused. He has never learned to communicate his innermost feelings. He has guarded them. Women need to communicate verbally so that they can feel attached to others. Men are content to be in the same room. Women interact.

One of the mid-life tasks is to include the opposite gender qualities into one's own being. Neugarten (1968) found that as men grew older they became more nurturing and gentle. Women were found to be more aggressive. Life is a process of integrating the whole self. When people can accomplish this task during mid-life, they grow and mature gracefully into older age.

Erikson (1950) suggests there is a sequence of eight psychosocial tasks that make up ego development across the life cycle. He believes that what is lost during a specific task impairs the development of the next stage or task. Levinson (1978) is more concerned about particular issues and concentrates on transitions. Reappraisal and changes in life structures characterize transitions.

Continuity and discontinuity are important concepts here. Crisis is experienced during periods of discontinuity. If development in mid-life is viewed as a normal process, then the emphasis is not on crisis. Change occurs and individuals become aware of who they are. If the emphasis is on discontinuities, then there is potential for crisis. This can occur in two ways.

If the developmental task involves a major negotiation of the relationship between self and identity, the process could be painful and stressful. It is difficult to give up the picture we have of ourselves and negotiate a new interaction between self and the world. Even if the old doesn't work any more, it is difficult to choose the unknown. The pain resulting from this type of change, if endured, can lead us to a more satisfying period in our lives. Developmental principles take into consideration the roles that an individual's personal history, motives, and choices play. Specific changes do occur across adult life.

An important unanswered question within the developmental model is, "Under what conditions are individuals able to attain adequate adult adjustment in spite of earlier developmental problems?" More attention needs to be paid to the social and cultural factors that affect the nature of change. Learn the ways change is experienced and negotiated. Realize the implications of change for personal well-being.

Life-Events Theory of Middle Age

A second theory or approach to mid-life is the life-events theory. Life events are described as identifiable changes in usual patterns of behavior. These changes can create stress. They also pose challenges to the individual to adapt to different ways of doing and responding. Usually included are work-related events such as retirement and getting fired or laid off, family-based events such as marriage, separation, divorce, widowhood, birth of children, and departure of children from parental home, and changes in finances, friendships, and life-style.

Traditionalists look at these changes from one perspective: the degree to which the changes disrupt established patterns of behavior. Changes will have varying degrees of impact on a person's well-being. Usually this depends on the amount of change that results from the event. Positive and negative events are both viewed as stressful.

Others see life events in a more complex way. They see more interaction between life changes and personal well-being. They look at both the meaning of the event for the individual and the personal social resources available to the individual. Both have some effect on how people respond to changing life events. Not all change is perceived as having the potential for crisis. There is enough room in this approach to separate events. Positive or non-consequential events have less negative effects on the individuals experiencing the event. Events that are perceived as negative or important produce stress.

Self-concept is a major variable in adulthood. Four dimensions of adult self-concept are found in the literature. The first involves an interpersonal dimension that focuses on social relationships. A second is an altruistic dimension that involves ethical, religious, and philosophical concerns. The third involves a sense of mastery and includes competence, a sense of well-being, creativity, and autonomy. The fourth is self-protectiveness, which includes physical and economical maintenance of well-being.

Life-Events Model

Major areas of change include family, work, health, finances, and friendships. Why change occurs is unclear in this particular model. Two types of change are identified (George, 1982). The first is voluntary. People choose to make changes. Choosing can lessen the stress involved in making the change. Nevertheless, there is still a certain amount of grieving that will occur. People are often not prepared for some of their emotional responses to change. They do not realize that whenever change occurs, some part of themselves is lost. People need to grieve that loss.

Involuntary change is more stressful. Results of involuntary change may be more negative. The stress and the grieving process involved in change may overwhelm people. They need to be aware of this. As a result, they will have to work harder to regain their equilibrium. Psychological losses include health, self-assessment, loss itself, and generativity.

TASKS OF MID-LIFE

Like every age and stage across the life span, mid-life involves certain tasks. The developmental and life-events models address processes and responses. The tasks are similar. The tasks most frequently mentioned in the literature are health, mortality, self-assessment, work, family, and social relationships.

The tasks addressed are a series of both internal and external activities during specific times during the life span. There is a certain universality about these tasks. Men and women continually identify these similar themes.

Mid-life is a relatively new field of study. Until rather recently, people died at a very early age compared with today's death rates. At the turn of the century, the average life span was about forty-five years of age. Control of childhood diseases, better child labor laws, better health care for expectant mothers, safer work environments, and changes in technology have contributed to longevity.

Losses in Mid-Life

Even though different tasks occur at different times across the life span, they can cause people problems. We do not easily change our behaviors or responses to situations. In fact, we become comfortable with the status quo.

There are normal changes that occur as people enter the mid-life transitional phase. Some of the changes are viewed as losses. For instance, health problems begin to surface. People may become alarmed and view these changes as negative. Whenever people involve themselves in self-assessment, losses occur. They lose some of what they liked about themselves so that they can become more of what they would like to become. Death, divorce, job change, and children growing into adulthood bring losses for mid-life people as well. Another loss involves generativity. Mid-life people realize that they are no longer the takers but the givers. Younger people look to them for leadership, answers, and insights.

Health Issues in Mid-Life

During mid-life, symptoms of physical decline appear. In their forties, men and women begin to experience weight redistribution, changes in eyesight, wrinkles, hair loss or graying, and diminished energy levels. All of these are normal, but in an extended life span they seem out of step with the rest of life. Men can respond to these changes by changing their lifestyles. They may become more involved in their work, family, or social activities, or they may seek the fountain of youth by drastically changing their appearance. They may also seek younger people to bolster their sense of youth. Actually, men are in a better position to continue to be accepted in society. Historically, women have suffered the double-edged sword of aging. Our culture highly esteems and respects attractiveness and beauty in women. As women in their middle years continue to experience changes in their appearance and energy levels, they can become less than acceptable to spouses and others within society. Sometimes middle-aged women give up their spouse and family for more freedom, but this happens less frequently than with men.

Mortality

It is in mid-life that people begin to be aware of their own mortality. This affects men more severely than it does women. People realize there is less time until death than from birth. Jaques (1965) suggests that men's struggle to come to terms with death is the primary task that defines middle age. Self-assessment, sex roles, and generativity become operative within individuals who have accepted their mortality.

Self-Assessment

This is the process of examining one's life. People ask themselves where they have been. The next question is, where are they going? Since mid-life signals a midpoint, what is to become of people and their remaining years? This process was used earlier in life, but its purpose was quite different. Then people wanted to know where they were in their career advancement, family planning, and specific life goals. As people continue through mid-life, they recognize that life is not black and white. They now realize that their wants and desires conflict with each other. They come to a point where they need to make choices. People cannot have it all. They begin to integrate the polarities mentioned earlier in this chapter.

Generativity

At mid-life, people begin to realize that they want to leave something for future generations. This can be abstract, for all mankind. It can also be more concrete, for their children or those for whom they are responsible at work. The problem is that if people do not work through their mid-life issues, they are in no position to contribute to others.

Levinson (1978) talks about reassessing the dream. Each person begins with a dream. This is essential. By mid-life, people can identify whether they have reached their dream. Often the dream is more than what people have attained; therefore, most will want to reassess. Those who replace the dream usually are happy or at least content with their lives to this point. Those who have not learned that life is give-and-take may still be concentrating on achieving the dream. They could very well feel that life has cheated them, has dealt them a bad hand. These people will continue to pursue what is not attainable. If they become disillusioned, they also run the chance of stagnating. They can easily arrest their growth. The results are very unhappy people who continue to move through life but do not participate in it.

Work, Family, and Social Relationships

The psychological tasks do affect people's work, family, and social relationships. The higher the satisfaction with one's own life, the better the quality of life is for those around the person.

Work. Work is an integral part of who people are and how they describe themselves. It is also their source of income, which allows them to live the life-style they have set for themselves. Men reach the peak in their occupations at mid-life. They come to a period where they decide to either continue to move up the occupational ladder or move unilaterally. With more mid-life people in the work force, the chances of continuing to move up are fewer. This can cause a major adjustment.

Until recently, as older persons moved out of the work force, there was room for middle-aged people to fill those spots. It was assumed there was something wrong when men were not continually promoted. Times change, but attitudes change more slowly. This is even more true of one's attitude about oneself. Others think no less of the person who is not promoted. The person himself could have a good deal of difficulty with this fact.

Middle-aged women traditionally have not occupied positions in the work force where promotion is available. If they worked, it was to add to the family income. The jobs they held were not a part of a career ladder. Few were employed in a professional capacity. Most followed the traditional mode of raising the children. Now, at mid-life, they want to return to school and follow a course of study that will lead to gainful employment. Often they establish career goals. Although they start at the bottom of the ladder, they can also experience a good deal of positive feedback. Their sense of self is enhanced.

This comes at a time when men have reached their peak. Men are in a position to relax and to take time away from the workplace. They begin to value family in a different way. If the wife is beginning to experience success in her career, she will want to put her time and energy there. This can cause problems within the marriage. If it does, then it also causes problems for the human resource specialist. Any stress outside the work force manages to influence workers on the job as well.

Family. As men face their issues at mid-life, families can suffer. Since the family is a unit, when one member faces a difficult situation, all are affected. The presence of teenage children compounds the issues. The teen years are difficult times to negotiate for children and parents. Sometimes children need and receive a good deal of time and attention. This may occur at the expense of their parents' relationship. Men may be trying to find their way. They establish a new dream and absorb the shocks of change in the work force or in their attitudes toward their work.

Women are facing the issue of what they want now that the children are almost grown. Traditionally, women were responsible for children and the home. Husbands did not have to concern themselves. They could concentrate on their careers. As more middle-aged women enter the work force, men find themselves in another position. They may for the first time find themselves responsible for home activities.

If men have come to terms with their work role, they will more easily adapt at home. If women realize that their changes can be threatening to others in the household, they can approach their changes differently. Together, all can experience more life satisfaction. There is a high correlation among job satisfaction, self-esteem, and home life.

Social Relationships. Social relationships across the life span differ for men and women. Men maintain more casual contacts and have more acquaintanceships. Women have more friendships. Since men are more competitive, they face fewer difficulties when they have no intimate relationships. Men traditionally learn to tough it out. They can do or be anything they want. Although this is not necessarily true, it is a goal middle-aged men try to achieve.

It is not clear whether men want and strive for more social interaction and relationships during mid-life. If they are content with their work and home life, there is a chance that they do. However, if they are in transition, they probably are spending all of their time and energy trying to make some sense out of their life. This is made more difficult if they have not developed intimate relationships. They then lack the necessary sounding boards to aide in figuring out their life. Men find it difficult to admit that they don't know how to do something. They also have difficulty expressing their needs and are often at a loss about what they want. A mid-life task is to sort out what one wants and how to achieve it. Others are necessary to provide the support mechanisms. If all of the social relationships men have are at the workplace, this could prove to be problematic. People who have adequate social relationships have higher self-esteem and can respond more positively to life's changes.

LOSSES IN MID-LIFE

Another aspect of mid-life is the realization of losses. When people gain something, they often lose something. Losses occur within oneself, within the environment that is society and workplace, and within the family. Sometimes the losses are not immediately replaced. Mid-life adults who grew up in dysfunctional families have had a chance to realize this, but this is a new experience for people who have had few problems. To meet these losses and move on, people need to learn grieving processes.

Losses happen across the life span, but they take on a special meaning during mid-life. People are in the process of evaluating their lives. They are beginning to give different meanings to family, work, and themselves. A recognition and acceptance of the finiteness of time causes part of this change. They are more aware that they will die. Some of the major losses incurred in mid-life involve work, family, and personal life.

Work-Related Losses

According to the U.S. Department of Commerce (1986), about 90 percent of middle-aged men and 60 percent of middle-aged women are in the work force. Traditionally, men continue in the work force through middle age. The increase in the number of women from about 40 percent reflects the influx of middle-aged women entering the work force.

Although middle-aged workers can lose their jobs, because of seniority they are at less risk than younger people. When they do lose their jobs, the impact is felt more intensely. There are two subgroups of unemployed. The first includes those whose layoffs are temporary. Shortage of work or the seasonal nature of the work causes these layoffs. People in this category will become employed within a six-month period and probably will return to the same type of job.

The second subgroup is displaced workers. These include people who have specific skills or have worked for one employer for a long time. Usually there is little chance that they will find work in their field of expertise. In either case, job loss during middle age can generate hardship. There can be occupational and economic problems. Occupations become obsolete every day. Although new occupations also come into being, these often need specialized training or the pay scale is less. Even if the person can reenter the work force in six months or less, the economic loss can be a setback. It can take a measurable amount of time to regain what was lost. There is the possibility that it can never be made up. Reentry women constantly meet this challenge.

Outplacement. This particular benefit is useful for mid-life people. It offers psychological assessment, career counseling, and job-hunting strategies for people who are put out of a job. Outplacement services are available within corporations or through the use of outside consulting firms. Outplacement became popular in the early 1960s when top managers began to use these services. The job losses resulted from mergers, acquisitions, and corporations that were streamlining their work force. Fortunately, the services are now extended to other displaced workers throughout organizations.

Losing a job can inflict harm to people's sense of self. This service, if utilized early, will provide the emotional support necessary. Workers need to reestablish their equilibrium as quickly as possible so that they can develop a job search plan of action. Outplacement service is not an employment agency. The outcome is not to find people jobs. Cole (1988) compares this service to a ritual: It helps people deal with an ending and gives them tools to move on to a beginning.

Outplacement services include helping people develop appropriate attitudes toward their job loss and their job search. People are taught job-search skills, resume-writing skills, and new coping skills, if necessary. Much of this is done in small group settings. If the number of participants in any one group is small enough and if there is sufficient follow-through, these groups work quite well. Individual members within the small groups share similar experiences. They become a support to one another by discussing techniques and stories and by offering encouragement to one another.

Besides learning how to find a new job, people have the opportunity to look at their talents and abilities. They may even discover that they no longer wish to work in the same area. They can explore new fields. Of course, financial security dictates how much time people can devote to this exploration. Again, you must note that outplacement services do not find employment for people. They give people the tools and support necessary to find employment. One of the major outcomes of this type of service is public relations, which can increase a positive image of the organization.

When referring people to outplacement counseling, you can give them several pointers.

1. Make sure that the outplacement service provides ongoing contact until the person is placed.
2. Ask for another counselor if not satisfied.
3. Ask for references of people who have been placed.
4. Be sure there is sufficient time spent on assessment.
5. Seek services that provide counseling for the entire family.

Other Problems Associated with Job Loss. Sometimes physical and mental health problems follow the loss of a job. The incurred stress can take its toll. Physical problems may mask the stress and make diagnosis difficult. It is not unusual for people who have lost their jobs to feel depressed or have other mental health problems. This is especially true for mid-life workers. Their chances of getting employment after a job loss are less than if they chose to change employment.

Interpersonal relations can also suffer. Men have a long history of equating what they do with who they are. Wives who are not employed outside the home could have their sense of self tied to the husband's occupation as well.

Personal Losses

Although work-related losses can be considered personal losses, they occur within a larger context. They can cause other losses, can change mid-life people's perspectives, or can be influenced by losses that are experienced in people's personal lives outside the work force. Some of the major personal losses that happen to people most frequently in mid-life are death, changes in the family structure, and aging parents.

Death. One loss that can occur during mid-life is the death of a spouse. Often this is the husband, which may force the widowed spouse to seek reentry into the work force. Sometimes the widow has not completed her grieving and this can affect her competency on the job. Time, patience, and understanding on the part of the human resource specialist and the worker's fellow employees can provide the reassurance the widow needs. If a wife dies, the husband may also throw himself into his work. Again, this is not healthy because he will not give himself the time necessary to complete his grief. He may be putting in long hours, but he may not be accomplishing anything. The human resource specialist can help by talking with the spouse and encouraging him to take time. It may even be necessary to suggest that he join a support group that deals with grief issues. If the organization has a human resource division with qualified personnel, suggest a visit. No one can make another person do anything. Sometimes the attitude and tone make a great deal of difference. Also, it is helpful to know enough about the person to be sure that he does not become unduly upset.

Another outcome of the loss of a spouse is that couples socialize with couples. If the widowed spouse does not have a support network of friends, the person will have to start over making friends. Couples do not usually continue to associate with the widowed spouse.

Changes in the Family Structure. At mid-life, changes occur within the family structure. This is referred to as the "empty nest" syndrome. For years this particular event was considered a woman's problem. However, when talking with women in mid-life whose children were leaving, researchers found their responses surprising. Most women were relieved they had completed their mothering. Although they felt some sadness, this can be attributed to normal grief that occurs whenever a major change happens. Men were found to experience more emotions during this time. This is understandable, since it is in mid-life that men begin to relax and take more time from their work. They are ready to get to know their children; however, the children are grown or gone.

Aging Parents. A relatively new phenomenon is the aging parent. With a greater percentage of people living longer, there is more chance that the mid-life worker will face aging parent issues.

Josephine has a reputation for being a conscientious worker. Lately her work is questionable. She is often late, takes more sick time, and is unpleasant to be around. She is referred to you. Josephine doesn't understand why she is receiving criticism for her work. She thinks she is doing as well as ever. She realizes that she is more tired than usual, but she attributes this to growing older.

When you ask her if anything has changed in her life, she thinks for a moment. Then she says that her mother-in-law moved in with her family. She is certain this isn't a problem. Although her mother-in-law needs a considerable amount of care, everyone pitches in to help. Depending on the amount of interaction you normally have with Josephine, you could ask a couple of more questions. The purpose of these questions is to get Josephine to think about the recent change in her routine and to determine if she is really as content with the situation as she seems. If Josephine still says that the mother-in-law is no problem, you will have to treat her as you would any unproductive employee. However, if Josephine begins to realize that this change could be an underlying cause of the change in her productivity, then you can suggest Josephine seek some help. It is not your place to know all there is to know about caring for an elderly person in the home. It is to your advantage, however, to know appropriate resources to recommend in these instances.

Often mid-life people who become responsible for their parents' care feel guilty if they complain. There is a common myth that we do not take care of our older people. In the good old days, children cared for their aging parents. Remember that at the turn of the century, the average age at death was about forty-five years. People did not live as long. If care was needed, it was for a shorter time. Today, when older people need care, it is usually more intense and for a longer duration. Adult parents can try to make their adult children feel guilty. "You will never put me in a home, will you?" "You will take care of me like I took care of grandma." Comments like these hold adult children hostage.

More mid-life women work today than ever before. Historically, women are the caregivers for their own relatives and their husband's as well. This puts a great deal of burden on the woman. Often women choose to leave the work force to respond to this need. It is difficult enough if it is the woman's mother, but it can become even more stressful if it is her mother-in-law. Increased stress from caregiving activities and financial changes can cause problems within the family.

How can some of these stresses be lessened? It is better for adult children to discuss long-term care with their parents if the parents need care. Neither children nor parents want to consider a long-term care facility, but sometimes that is the best solution. Families and family homes are not set up to accommodate an extended family member.

There are several viable options if adult children wish to continue to care for their parents. Among these are adult day-care centers or home health agencies. Corporations are looking at adult day-care facilities. They recognize it is more economical to provide this service than to lose their employees. They also realize that this mid-life loss is stressful to their employees.

Although not every loss has been identified, these should give you a sense of what can be going on in the day-to-day lives of your employees. You may also notice that when losses or changes occur, people seem to react or respond differently. They may be going through a transitional process.

TRANSITIONS

Transitions are normal processes that occur across the life span. If they are normal and can happen at any age, why include them? Most people are unaware that they are experiencing transition. We did not learn to identify these processes from an early age.

There are stages within the transitional process, as well as unidentified feelings and experiences. When people realize that most of what they are going through is normal, they can spend their energy completing the transition.

The process of transition includes change, and losses are a part of change. There are anticipated or unanticipated changes. When employees choose to make a change, they experience more control over their experiences and feelings. However, they may enter periods of discomfort, self-doubt, and even depression.

Anticipated Transitions

Charles spent a couple of years evaluating his life. He decided he had to make several changes so that he could get on with his life. First, he had to reestablish meaning within his marriage or end it. Second, he needed to change his job or his career. The family members knew Charles was experiencing some difficulty but were unaware of the cause. He did not share his thoughts with anyone else. His philosophy was to solve the problem and then tell others involved about his decisions. But, transitions take time and affect others. When Charles announces his decisions, he is well into the process. He is anticipating some of the responses to his decisions. However, all other members of his family and his coworkers will face unanticipated transitions.

For the sake of clarification, let's assume that Charles decided the marriage is over. He tells his wife. He may even wonder why she has trouble accepting what he has to say. The person who makes the decision has an advantage over the person who receives the message. Charles may be at point five while his wife is at point one. The children will also be at point one. Charles may seem very calm and self-assured while everyone else is in shock.

Charles also decides to sell his share of the partnership and start a new business. His two partners were aware that Charles was preoccupied, but they thought it was because of the new client they were approaching. This is a crucial time in the organization; any major change of direction could affect its ability to attract new customers. Again, Charles' actions forced others into a transitional process.

Transition as a Process

People do not control their lives. Events, circumstances, and other people affect our lives. Sometimes all we can do is try to control our responses to situations. Unanticipated transitions make this difficult because we are blind sighted.

Schlossberg (1987) talks about another type of transition, which is caused by anticipated events that never occur. Parents at mid-life may have had expectations that do not materialize. They may have anticipated that when the children were grown, the couple's life together would be better, but it isn't. Husbands and wives may have expected to live their middle years with their spouse, but the spouse dies, or divorces them. They may have looked forward to financial security, but some outside event takes their savings and leaves them near poverty. There appears to be stress related to events that are expected but never happen.

According to Bridges (1980), transitions involve three steps or stages. The first step is an ending, followed by a neutral zone and finally a beginning. Countless numbers of mid-life people who became familiar with this process found that the three stages helped them understand what they were experiencing.

Endings. Often people begin another job, career, or life-style without closing the door on the previous experience. To begin, one needs to end. How do people know they haven't really ended the previous situation? One way is to test their feeling level. If they are dissatisfied or unsure of the present, they may have unresolved issues. Or they may start something new only to find themselves failing. Divorced people who experience hostility and anger long after the event would do well to examine whether they have let go. Usually when an ending is completed, people can let go and begin their new lives. Sometimes, because the event was unanticipated, people become stuck with their negative feelings. They waste a good deal of time and energy wishing it hadn't happened, placing blame, feeling sorry for themselves, or plotting revenge. All of these activities prove to be futile. People end up hurting themselves. They become less productive, are less involved in their work, and could be making costly mistakes.

Endings do not resolve themselves overnight. This too is a process, and processes take time. There is a certain amount of grieving that needs to take place. While this is going on, people will not be themselves. Others, because of their own discomfort, may encourage them to hurry along. People need to come to terms with the event that has caused the ending. They need to recognize and deal with the feelings they have. Sometimes extra help is essential. Others, once they know their responses are normal, can move on by themselves.

Neutral Zone. The second stage in the transition process is the neutral zone. All people have experienced this sometime during their lives. This is a place where nothing seems to happen. People have the sensation that they are walking on eggs. They feel that whenever they put one foot down, everything changes. They feel they are not on firm ground. There is a purpose for this period of time. It is the time to sort, evaluate, and dream. Since it is so uncomfortable, people try to move through this stage as quickly as possible. But there is no hurrying this stage. It takes as long as it takes. Rushing through could cause people to abort the process or make changes that are not in their best interest.

Often, feelings similar to those experienced in the neutral zone give clues to employees about their jobs. Change occurs when the old things don't work any more. If you have workers who work without energy or zest, one of the reasons could be that they are experiencing an ending. They do not receive the same kind of fulfillment from their work. They may even have given up and are riding it out. They are into the neutral zone but do not know what the next step is. Rather than use negative procedures with these people, you would do better to talk with them. One of the outcomes of an ending and the neutral zone is a return to old things in new ways. Perhaps these workers need some change but do not need to change organizations. With a little time and energy, you could save yourself some very valuable mid-life workers. If they are in a work-related transition, it would be advantageous to point them in a direction to get some help. Even if they choose to leave, they will leave with positive feelings about your organization.

Beginnings. If people use the neutral zone, they will know when it is time to begin. They will recognize the right move. If the change is dramatic, people may experience feelings of being overwhelmed. If they remember to take things one step at a time, they will overcome these feelings in time. Change is present as long as people are alive. Nothing remains the same. Either we progress or we regress.

Mid-life is a time of constant change. Sometimes the change borders on crisis, and at other times it happens in a smooth, reasonable fashion. Usually there is no change without some pain. The minimum of pain comes with the grieving process. We grieve the loss of who we were along with the excitement of who we are becoming. Whether this change happens because of changes in the workplace or at home, people's behavior changes. We cannot divide ourselves easily between work and home.

ORGANIZATIONAL RESPONSE

Companies and organizations are utilizing employee assistance programs as interaction with workers becomes more diversified. What are EAPs? Why do they exist? What do they accomplish? These are three important questions that need to be answered. Human resource specialists have this responsibility. They are charged to some degree with meeting the profit-making goals of the organization. They achieve this through working with employees. You, the human resource specialist, are often called on when employees are not producing. The organization looks for a return on its investment in human resources. Although it is not well reported in financial statements, organizations spend much of their revenue on their workers. The human resource specialist is responsible for hiring, firing, complying with the Equal Employment Opportunity Commission (EEOC) standards, and more. You need to be aware of areas that affect productivity. The company profits when its employees are productive. Companies cannot make profits if their employees are not producing.

The realization has grown that employees are an integral part of the success of the organization. It has become apparent that employees who are experiencing problems are costing the company money. Firing the employees with problems proved to be costly. Today, rather than fire them, organizations are implementing the concept of employee assistance programs.

What Are EAPs?

Employee assistance programs are free, confidential, professional services designed to help employees and their families resolve personal problems. The programs are confidential and voluntary. They provide people with opportunities to find help through the assistance of professionals.

Thus far, there is little consistency among the EAPs, but they do have a common purpose. They provide a serious, positive response to the negative influence in workers' lives. EAPs relieve human resource specialists and supervisors of fulfilling the inappropriate role of counselor. They provide a mechanism to help keep valuable workers and, in some instances, help reduce health care costs.

There are three basic models for providing this service. The first is in-house. When a company has a large number of employees, it is to its advantage to hire and finance a staff to conduct this service. The second is to contract with an outside provider. A company uses this method because it is too small to warrant its own staff and because an outside provider insures confidentiality. The third is as a member of a consortium of businesses that collectively serve a sufficient number of people. All members of the consortium contribute financially on a per-employee basis.

Basic Components

Usually every EAP has the following components. It assists the employer in developing and implementing a policy. Managers and supervisors are trained to recognize troubled employees. There is a minimum of diagnosis and then referral. If outside community resources are used, EAP monitors evaluate the services and provide educational seminars identifying issues that influence job performance. People involved in EAPs know insurance carriers and benefit policies, so referrals can benefit from these.

Why Do EAPs Exist?

Increased demands from daily living influence people's interaction at home and within the work force. The cost of carrying employees with problems undermines the long-term goals of the organization. Problems that arise at home often cause poor job performance. Personal problems can lead to increased absenteeism, reduced quality and quantity of production, and poor attitudes toward work.

Sometimes, if caught early enough, home problems can be addressed before they carry over to the work force. If the problems are more serious, they can cause major interruptions within the workplace. Employees with problems can disrupt fellow workers, as well as other workers' productivity.

Scope of the Problem. Most of us would probably feel more comfortable if we could dismiss the notion that what happens at home influences the workplace. It would certainly make people's lives a little easier, or so it seems. Television, movies, newspapers, journals, and magazines bring us face to face with problems people are constantly facing. Movies on television show spouse abuse, addictive behaviors, and dysfunctional family systems. Names and phone numbers are given so that people who recognize these problems in their lives can call to get help. Articles appear in journals and magazines listing clues and giving examples. Newspapers carry articles about these abuses occurring in small towns and large cities.

Statistics tell us that about 10 to 12 percent of the work force is addicted to alcohol. Drug usage by adults is not a small matter either. There are indications that the peak prevalence of depression is during middle age. There are stresses from society coupled with increased pressure from the job and from parental roles. Family violence or family problems involving abuse, finances, and normal transitions to mid-life affect home and work life.

EAPs began by addressing alcohol and drug problems. Many still offer only these limited services. Others have expanded to also offer referrals for marital and family, financial, and psychological problems. Some organizations have special programs for their executives and top management. Although company executives may back an EAP in their organization, the program is established for rank-and-file workers. They recognize that need but fail to realize that they themselves could profit from the same kind of help (Golden, 1989).

Financial Impact

Employees with problems cost companies money. They undermine productivity and cause stress for you, the human resource specialist. There is more absenteeism among employees with problems. It is suggested that the rate is up to six times more than for the average employee. Fire, hire, and train is an option, but this too can be very costly for the company. Often mid-life employees are very valuable. They have proven themselves but are temporarily unable to complete their commitments in a productive manner. Cost-efficiency studies indicate that it is less expensive for the company to invest dollars in EAPs than to fire, hire, and train.

Employees with problems also increase risks to safety. Statistics show that about 15 percent of on-the-job accidents are a result of personal problems. People become preoccupied with their problems and fail to take the necessary safety precautions. These on-the-job accidents may involve machinery, or loss of business through rudeness, or failure to complete work for clients.

Benefits

Employees with problems make up the majority of discipline problems and compensation claims and a large share of medical care costs. An effective employee assistance program within the organization can help minimize the negative effects of problems that employees experience. If used effectively, EAPs can address work and personal problems that occur outside the work force.

Companies who have used EAPs report a significant increase in productivity and a sizable drop in absenteeism. These two items together make a noticeable difference. The bottom line is to make a profit. Companies cannot spend time and energy both sorting out problems caused by employees and making a profit. A well-functioning EAP using skilled personnel can aid problem employees in identifying what kind of help they need and where they can get it.

As a result, individual employees can improve their self-image and self-concepts, can be more productive, and can enhance their own sense of morale. As more and more individual employees' morale is raised, so is that of the work force as a group. Another benefit that hasn't been mentioned is an increased sense of pride, trust, and loyalty toward the organization. This in turn increases the organization's contributions within a community. The public relations gains certainly can be only an asset to the organization.

HUMAN RESOURCE SPECIALISTS TAKE NOTE

Employee assistance program managers and personnel need to work very closely with you, and you with them. There are some handy hints that can aid this process. First, recognize that if any of your employees have problems, the problems can become worse. It is to your advantage to recognize clues and make referrals to the EAP. Always talk in private with employees, and be sure that EAP personnel do the same. Privacy and confidentiality are essential if the process is to work effectively. Communicate the company's concern for work performance. Remind employees with problems that their personal problems can and do affect the total organization. Often people feel they are just a cog in the wheel. They think that no one notices them and that they have no impact on the organization. If you are responsible for referring, remember to explain the employee assistance program as it operates within your organization. Emphasize that employees decide whether or not to use the service.

Employees still need to know that they are responsible for their actions. If their problems necessitate disciplinary action, these procedures are still in effect. Having problems does not absolve employees from the repercussions. However, if they decide to seek help through an EAP, there is some room for different types of responses.

Job performance documentation is fundamental from the outset of an employee's affiliation with the organization. It becomes essential if the employee begins to experience problems. Be specific about what the company will or will not tolerate. When this is clearly stipulated, employees can make informed choices. You also can make difficult decisions more easily.

Do not diagnose or try to solve employees' personal problems. Talk about problems that are apparent within the workplace, but do not probe personal problems. Do not moralize or lecture. There are well-defined rules and behaviors. Show employees where they meet these and where they fall short. Do not be tempted to excuse them or cover up for them. People with problems will not benefit if others take away their responsibility for their actions.

Do not allow employees with problems to pull your sympathy chain. They may want to tell you their stories. Resist. If you have documented their work performance, you can continually refer to the facts. This may sound heartless, but when people are hired, they enter an agreement with the organization. They agree to produce in exchange for payment.

Referral Process

Employees can be referred in several different ways. If there is no change after you have brought a complaint to an employee's attention, you can refer the employee to the EAP. If employees confide a personal problem to you, again it is in your best interest to refer them to EAP.

Employees can also refer themselves. They can be referred by coworkers, family members, friends, or people in the community. The earlier the problem is identified and the person referred, the easier it is to deal with the situation. The longer the problem persists, the greater the probability that the employee's performance on the job will suffer.

Some of the theories and tasks of mid-life have been explored. By now you may have realized that not all problem employees are beyond help. Some of these mid-life people are going through normal changes that occur within this particular stage in life. Changing the description from problem employee to employees with problems can lead to different types of responses from you and the organization.

5

The Dysfunctional Workplace

This chapter will identify and describe the dysfunctional workplace and the dysfunctional organization. Information and examples will be given showing how these workplaces and organizations contribute to producing and enhancing dysfunctional employees. The concept of burnout will be addressed, as well as the impact of layoffs and terminations. A view of the possibility of incorporating learning cultures within the organization will be discussed. Finally, the role you, the human resource specialist, can play will be explored.

CHARACTERISTICS OF DYSFUNCTIONALS

A workplace can be dysfunctional in one or more of the three following areas: top executives, managers, and rank-and-file employees. There are several reasons why an organization or a workplace becomes dysfunctional. One is dysfunctional operational objectives; another is external pressure and stress caused by either the market economy or personal problems. Addictive personalities and failure to address issues of drug and alcohol abuse among the employees also contribute to workplace dysfunction.

Job documentation is the most effective and the only legitimate way to refer people to employee assistance programs or other types of counseling. Diagnosis and treatment are out of your realm of expertise and knowledge. Inappropriate involvement could lead to legal complications. If managers or employees have problems, these will eventually surface and affect the job. This can be a double-edged sword. By the time the problems show themselves in the work, they may be rather advanced and require a major intervention. You will also need to document job performance to be able to show decline, disciplinary actions, and the like.

There is a way to move more quickly once job performance is affected. Continuous disciplinary actions, discussions, or dismissals are time-consuming and counterproductive. But if you are aware of warning signs and clues, you will not be blind-sighted. Knowledge of the warning signs of codependent behavior, substance abuse, and dysfunctional personalities is an advantage. You will be able to identify problems while you talk with employees. This is a time-saving element that puts you in a position to offer referrals to alternative services.

Remember, confidentiality is vital. This should be broken only if employees express dangerous, threatening intentions toward themselves or others. Then notify the appropriate person at the workplace, the family, a member of the EAP staff, and if necessary, an enforcement person.

CHARACTERISTICS OF A
DYSFUNCTIONAL ORGANIZATION

There are two major elements present in a dysfunctional organization. The first, denial, is expected because this is also one of the difficulties addictive people face. Addicts and dysfunctional people deny that there is a problem. The second element concerns process. When dysfunctional behavior surrounds people, that is the only behavior they know. This is their reality. Those who have other ways of behaving or responding readily see the inappropriate behavior.

People run organizations. People carry out the day-to-day work. If the people who head organizations are dysfunctional, they will incorporate the same attitudes and behaviors in their business as well. The top executives affect the entire organizational system. The whole organization responds to and even takes on the personality of the top executives.

Schaef and Fassel (1988) identify several characteristics of addicts and suggests that these are present in dysfunctional organizations as well. The first is denial. If it doesn't exist, there is no problem. The top executives meet to discuss the corporation. The meeting takes place at a posh resort. Although the reason for the meeting was to take stock, the message was to have fun and relax. Stated organizational objectives are at odds with the implied purpose of the meeting. All work and no play makes Jack a dull boy. Adam is responsible for personnel matters. He has looked forward to this meeting because there are several serious problems with three managers. Again, his report is last on the agenda. By this time, the group is eager to get on with the fun and entertainment. Even though Adam has an effective presentation prepared, everyone is restless. The consensus is that Adam is making a mountain out of a molehill. Time will take care of the problems he has identified. If the problems still exist at the time of the next meeting, there are three possibilities. The managers may be given a reprimand, called in to discuss the problem, or fired. Denial: There may be a problem, but it is small and will probably go way by itself.

Confusion is another characteristic of dysfunctional organizations. Everyone spends a good deal of time and energy figuring out what is going on. Confusion deflects responsibility. Some organizations thrive on confusion and crisis. Nothing is ever accomplished, and no one is responsible. Let's go back to Adam and his problem. The three managers who worried Adam have gone over his head. They are in collusion: They want Adam replaced. They gain the ear of other executives because dysfunctional people can be very charming and can become experts at conning others. They shift the blame for poor production, ineffective communication, and low morale to Adam, and they criticize his management style. Everyone is confused. Things are working, but no one is sure why or sure who is responsible.

Self-centeredness is a predominant characteristic within an addictive organization. Dysfunctional people need to be the center of attention. They will do anything congruent with the intensity of their problem to get and maintain that position.

Dishonesty is another common characteristic of addictive behavior. Active addicts are master con artists. They are dishonest with themselves, with others around them, and with the world at large. Sometimes, the purpose of this dishonesty is to avoid facing their feelings. The outcome of this dishonesty is confusion. We face dishonesty all the time. Some companies want to sell their product and perfect the packaging to deflect the consumer from questioning. Dishonesty can become the norm. People instinctively know not to believe advertising, product guarantees, agreements, or promises.

This leads to the scarcity model. In this model, there is not enough to go around. Quantity becomes more important than quality. More of everything becomes the norm. More armaments, larger gross national product, more money, and more control fuel the scarcity model. Corporate executives who espouse this model stress company loyalty. The way to get ahead in these corporations is to sacrifice one's personal life, values, and beliefs for the sake of the organization. Rewards are based on the amount of business brought into the company. How executives obtain this business is never questioned. Success is the key word.

Rewards are also based on the promise of what will be fulfilled tomorrow. The ones who make the promises and build expectations rarely, if ever, fulfill those promises. By the time people realize this, they have sacrificed so much it may even be difficult for them to admit they bought into a false set of expectations. They begin to believe that tomorrow everything will be different. This is especially true when corporate heads continue to flash new promises and sidestep the broken promises. Excuses and denial are part of the escape route.

Invalidation is a process used by corporate executives who are dysfunctional. The result is to discredit everyone else's ideas, suggestions, solutions, knowledge, and feelings. People who use this process acknowledge other frames of reference but do not accept them. They protect themselves and bolster their own egos in several ways. They must always be right, better than others, and have all the correct solutions to problems (Pace, 1989). This process does not allow information, data, and the combined knowledge of the group to surface. Sometimes people who are the best deflectors and invalidators are also charismatic. How can one who seems to see the future so clearly and has such a large following be so off target? As people try to answer this question for themselves, they become confused. Ambivalence results.

It takes very skilled people to see through the facade and realize that this particular type of charismatic leader is also dysfunctional. Convincing others is a difficult task. A good deal of harm may result before people put together all the pieces of this puzzle. Sometimes the mere enormity of identifying and attempting to solve the problem keeps people from stating the obvious.

Conflicting Goals and Directives

There is a red flag that can alert people to dysfunctional organizations. The problem is that it takes time before sufficient information and activities surface. The dysfunctional organization hires using one agenda and then operates from another agenda. The philosophy and stated goals impress people. They are elated to be hired as a member of an organization that matches their values and beliefs. However, there comes a time when the new hires discover incongruence and begin to question inconsistencies. What they thought they would be doing or how they thought they were to act is different from the reality. Eventually, they may feel they were misled, which is not a pleasant thing to experience. The anger, hostility, and feelings of being used can distort the situation. It takes time to sort out what is really going on and what part the newly hired people themselves play in the whole scenario.

Congruence is essential for healthy people to function at their best. It is difficult to get a dysfunctional organization to admit there is a difference between stated and operational agendas. These organizations have crossed over the line and now believe their own con. People who work in this type of organization need to change their perception of it. They need to realize that what they see, hear, and feel is accurate; they then can make a decision about their future. Often, employees question themselves and decide that they are wrong; they then change to fit the organization. This leads to dysfunctional behavior by these employees. The corporation continues to operate, and the workers eventually become loyal to it regardless of its dishonesty.

Another clue to dysfunctional organizations is communication that is often indirect, vague, confused, and ineffective. Written and verbal messages lose their value as they channel through several interpretations. The original meaning or intent is obscured by the time the messages are received at the end of the line. There may also be a lot of written communication. The more complex the process, the more the ineffectiveness is masked.

Human resource specialists gauge the level of dysfunctional behavior within an organization. A rule of thumb equates the amount of gossip with the level of dysfunction. Executives and managers use triangles to send messages from one person to another through a third. Secrets are also predominant. No one knows for sure what the facts are. Everything is kept silent.

If top executives meet to clarify and solve problems but get no where, the organization may be having problems. When people are afraid or unwilling to be direct and give their input, they may be trying to avoid conflict. The problem is that conflict is a part of life. The sooner we learn how to manage conflict, the sooner we can address major problems and situations. There are corporations that cannot tolerate direct communication, honesty, or differing points of view.

Serious problems arise when dysfunctional organizations lose sight of their reason for existing. The dysfunctional organization mirrors behaviors of dysfunctional people. These organizations may take on new ventures without ever referring back to the reason for their existence. They seek the quick fix, or at least temporary relief from existing problems. Personnel within a dysfunctional organization are either dysfunctional or run the risk of becoming dysfunctional. Corporate executives may be dysfunctional or not. They may be completely healthy in their own right and yet manage to hire or promote people who are dysfunctional. This is a hallmark of a well-developed con job.

Dysfunctional Managers

At times, the major problems that arise between employees and managers lie in the way that each perceives the job to be done. Some people catch on and respond very quickly. Others need more time to digest the idea and learn and respond to the process, and they work more slowly. If the boss is a quick thinker and works quickly as well, there may be a conflict with employees who are slower. This can be a simple problem of communication. Talking together can often solve this problem before it gets out of hand.

Matejka and Dunsing (1989) point out a situation where the problem could be more difficult to handle. He talks about larger organizations where conflict arises between departments or between individuals within departments. Sending mixed messages or being unnecessarily competitive can be detrimental. Sometimes these differences arise from expectations placed on them by others. For instance, in the factory part of the organization, the cleaning crew is not expected to keep everything dust free. Charlie, who worked in this department for several years, was transferred to clean offices. He didn't pay attention to dusting office furniture or cleaning the coffee urns. Charlie's work disappoints his new supervisor because, after all, Charlie came with great references and praise. Expectations had changed, but no one informed Charlie. He knew his work was unsatisfactory, but he wasn't sure of the reason. This too is simple to handle once those in charge know the source of the problem.

Managers, like the rest of us, want similar things. They often work to preserve the status quo, want to save face, and protect their turf (Matejka & Dunsing, 1989). Employees can respond to this type of leadership by sharing information with them and negotiating.

Managers with Personality Problems. Rank-and-file employees are not the only ones who can have personality problems. Sometimes people are promoted or hired who are not as mentally healthy as they seemed. Robert was well liked by his fellow workers. He cheered them on and helped raise the morale of the group. As a result, he earned a promotion. Soon afterward, Robert seemed to change. When employees came to him with their problems, he became overwhelmed. He had to make hard decisions that left people feeling unhappy with him. He even heard from the grapevine that some employees did not like him. As he worried more about not being liked, he was unable to make any decisions. People stopped going to him with problems or for advice. The unit was failing to meet its quota. Employees were wasting time talking about Robert and about each other. They no longer had any direction. They also did not have their fellow worker, Robert, to provide guidance.

Golden (1989) makes an important distinction. There is a difference between managers with personality problems and those with emotional problems. Emotional problems are usually short-term. Mid-life workers can be expected to experience some emotional problems as they move through this period's transitions. Divorce, death, and family or financial problems can also cause some concern. If people are secure and have a good sense of self, they will be able to get themselves back on track in a short while. If they are not, they will seek help.

Personality problems are more difficult to handle. Since these are an integral part of a person, they are harder to identify and then to change. There is more resistance because we are talking about a part of the total person. Often these personality problems began in early childhood and have continued. They may even have been rewarded in the past. They may never have been challenged.

Golden (1989) identifies several personality problems that managers may have. He suggests that these problems are kept under control until something changes and stress increases. When these managers experience change, they can take on a variety of behaviors. Some managers may exhibit aggression and have loyalty only for themselves. Others may lie or distort the truth. Still others may become chronically depressed, anxious, or hyperactive. There is the manager who trusts no one and the one who belittles employees to impress others. Others become the abusive manager, the compulsive manager, or the stew-stirrer manager.

The negative effects resulting from a problem manager are costly for organizations. They are also difficult to determine because other reasons can be given to explain the effects.

One of the more easily tracked negative effects is high turnover. When employees in certain units or areas are being replaced frequently, questions arise. Often, problem managers are crafty. They use any means available to shift the blame from themselves to others. Employees who leave under these conditions may be reluctant to talk about the reasons. They do not wish to harm their chances for other employment. The workers who choose to leave are often those who are the most valuable to the organization. Finding any other position is not difficult for them. They may prefer to leave without identifying the reasons. A high degree of turnover is costly to an organization, since training workers to fill specific roles within an organization is expensive. That is why it is worthwhile to spend a little time and energy finding the reason for this turnover.

Absenteeism is another costly outcome. Employees may choose to miss work rather than quit and find another job. High absenteeism in any unit reflects the possibility of high stress. A healthy organization investigates the causes of this stress. If the manager is causing the stress, the problem may be overlooked at first. Other managers within the organization may be reluctant to expose the manager with problems. Although at first glance this seems farfetched, it happens all the time. Peer pressure or a perceived threat to a career could cause others to excuse, overlook, or rationalize the problem manager's behavior.

The longer problem managers continue, the more likely it is that the better employees will leave. Those who remain may have problems themselves. They may be all too happy to continue working in a situation where they can coast along. They may be close to retirement and have little investment in the present job. They may also have no commitment to work after retirement. Those healthy employees who stay can become dysfunctional themselves. It is difficult to work in an unhealthy environment without falling prey to similar attitudes and behaviors.

Chemically Dependent Managers. When a manager's irrational behaviors are compounded by drug or alcohol abuse, all those who work with the manager are subjected to greater stress. This has a twofold outcome. Those employees who are relatively healthy will choose maladaptive coping mechanisms, such as absence, turnover, increased illness, and possibly sabotage, low productivity, or other dysfunctional behaviors. Those employees who are substance abusers may increase their intake. Employees who are dysfunctional could react more often and with more extreme behavior. The costs to the organization, although not easily calculated, are enormous.

The substance-abusing manager is not likely to take advantage of employee assistance programs. This is especially true if the manager's superiors look askance at such a program or believe the program is only for rank-and-file employees. A second outcome is that substance-abusing managers will be very unlikely to refer subordinates for treatment. If they expose others, they may feel that they too will be exposed. A whole unit or area can be severely damaged as a result. Studies indicate that as many as 25 percent of any given work force suffers from the effects of substance abuse, including abuse by employers, employees, and others. The National Institute on Drug Abuse estimates that the costs are more than $100 billion annually.

DYSFUNCTIONAL ORGANIZATIONS' IMPACT ON EMPLOYEES

There are at least three ways employees can interact dysfunctionally. First, they may have been dysfunctional before they entered the work force. Second, they may be going through a particularly difficult transition and may appear to be more dysfunctional than they really are. Or third, the organization may be dysfunctional. In this case, employees utilize or adopt dysfunctional behavior to survive.

Diamond and Allcorn (1990) present an interesting theory about manager-subordinate relationships. They suggest that all employees enter organizations with some sense of their own personal value, commonly referred to as self-esteem. The employees also have a certain ego strength that represents the quality of their self-cohesiveness. When critical events happen, employees respond based on the strength of their self-esteem and ego strength. Since employees have varying degrees of each, they will respond differently. When normal anxiety is present, those with an adequate sense of self will be able to handle it. Problems arise when this sense of self is inadequate.

Those who become neurotically anxious respond to stress with exaggerated, inappropriate, and compulsive behaviors. Employees who have an idealized self-image attempt to control events and feelings. They may become narcissistic, arrogant, and vindictive and may use triangles and gossip to help themselves regain their inflated sense of self. Employees who have a repressed self-image will withdraw from the situation.

When stress is not present, these tendencies are hidden. They come to the forefront only when situations are perceived as stressful. Managers can also have these types of behavior. If they respond in a maladaptive manner, their subordinates are affected. The effect on well-adjusted employees might be less, but the maladjusted employee is placed at greater risk.

It is important to be able to identify the events that the employees perceive as critical and thereby stressful. Managers and employees need to recognize their patterns of response and those of others. When people feel a threat to their own sense of self, they consciously or unconsciously use defense mechanisms to regain a sense of equilibrium. Diamond and Allcorn (1990) have devised a rather extensive model that describes the interactions among various types of managers and their subordinates. If you have recognized problems but are unsure of the interaction, you would find "The Freudian Factor" very informative.

We have talked at length about middle-aged employees who were never challenged about their misbehavior. As a result, they continue their dysfunctional behavior. We have also addressed the issue of transitions. Midlife brings with it an assortment of changes that can throw people off their guard. They can become dysfunctional until they are able to make the necessary decisions, changes, and adjustments.

Dysfunctional organizations put unrealistic demands on their employees. These may go unnoticed until mid-life, when people begin to look closely at their work life. Bridges (1980) indicates that mid-life workers often make a shift from becoming more specialized in their field to broadening out and diversifying their knowledge. This is similar to no longer wanting to climb the occupational ladder. Often employees know by mid-life that they are competent at what they do. They want to move toward learning why rather than how.

It is not unusual to hear comments like the following: "If you are a company person, then you will be willing to work 60 or 70 hours a week." "You are to be ready at a moment's notice." "The company comes first, then your personal life." "If you do this, you will be rewarded." These are some of the strategies that managers use to manipulate the person on the way up the ladder. Unfortunately or perhaps fortunately, mid-life people who are responding positively to their mid-life transitions think twice before accepting the company line. They probably have already experienced the emptiness of the management's promise of future rewards. They are not bitter or unhappy; they are realistic.

There are those mid-life people who become dysfunctional to maintain their position in the work force. Those employees who believe the promises of the organization may pass the point of no return. They may be people who were taught that the workplace is like a family. They look forward to getting their approval, sense of self, and caring from their fellow workers and their managers. They may also rely on their work to provide their social interactions. Companies could in fact emphasize the family spirit. Schaef and Fassel (1988) found in the companies studied that people who were reluctant to view their workplace as family often did not stay with the company very long. Those who perceived the organization like a family found interactions that occur in nuclear families also occur in organizations.

Often, organizations that promote the family spirit do so out of the need for power and control. This is not unlike family structures as well. Step out of line and suffer the consequences.

Workaholism can be a direct result of employees' needs. Dysfunctional organizations reward those who work long hours and show extreme dedication to the organization. This can assist employees by cloaking and maintaining their dysfunctional behavior. It can keep them from admitting their weaknesses and resolving personal conflicts. If they are so appreciated at work, why is everyone else disturbed with them? It cannot be their fault.

Workaholics have the same characteristics and behaviors of other addictive people. Robinson (1989), himself a recovering workaholic, talks about brownouts. He describes these as a high that results from work. He suggests that workaholics suffer memory losses of trips and conversations because they are preoccupied with their work. They have the ability to tune everything else out. They also have an acceptable excuse. In our competitive world, people are encouraged to spend an inordinate amount of time and energy focusing on work—encouraged, applauded, and rewarded. Work addicts spend a lot of time mentally planning and thinking about future events. Concentration on the future allows people to be free of the past and the present. How can anyone point a finger at someone who is so dedicated? Of course, the marriage and family suffer. If workaholics are not married, their social and personal lives suffer. There is evidence that the increase in the number of women alcoholics is a result of overworking. Women, especially single women, are not taking time for themselves. Since they focus completely on work, they are not taking care of themselves. They are burning out.

Sheila commutes an hour to and from work each day. She begins her workday at 7:30 A.M., which means she is out of her apartment by 6:15. She usually finishes her workday at about seven in the evening. She arrives home about eight or later. By this time she is too tired to cook. She has a glass of wine to unwind. It isn't long before the glass becomes several glasses. As this routine continues over time, Sheila takes less and less care of herself. She is well on her way to having major problems.

BURNOUT IN THE WORKPLACE

Burnout can be a result of a dysfunctional organization's impact on employees. It also can be a result of dysfunctional employees' interactions. White (1986) addresses the complex nature of burnout, describing it as resulting from "the complex interrelationships between the vulnerability of individual workers, the conditions and processes in the work environment, and the relationships of both workers and the organization with the outside ecosystem" (p. 6).

In time, the stress of a particular situation begins to undermine the particular defense mechanism we use to respond to stress. When this happens, inappropriate responses take over. Some of the more prominent are paranoia, decreased emotional control, a sense of feeling crazy, and feelings of hopelessness, loneliness, or being trapped. Other inappropriate responses include anxiety or fear, blaming, martyrdom, anger, detachment, or intellectualizing.

Anyone can experience one or several of these responses on occasions. Mid-life people undergoing a transition will quickly recognize some of these characteristics in themselves as they read through the list. *Intensity* and *frequency* are key words when attempting to identify whether oneself or others in the organization are burning out.

The more dysfunctional the organization, the more frequently people will experience the symptoms of burnout. In fact, White proposes that people who are employed by closed-system organizations probably experienced closed family systems as well. Healthy people who recognize the symptoms of burnout will seek help to identify the reasons why they are burning out and will take steps to alter the situation. Those people who know only a closed system will continue to operate in spite of being burned out. They will cause major problems for organizations that conduct themselves in a less rigid style. You will need to know enough about your organization to be able to identify whether it is a closed system. If it is, then you will find it difficult to provide the support services necessary to reduce burnout. You may be fortunate enough to work within an organization that is itself healthy, one that has a goal of keeping and strengthening its employees. Your task, though difficult, becomes easier. You will have the support necessary to direct those who need help.

A Sense of Self

A healthy sense of self empowers individuals. Organizations that recognize this make a positive contribution to their employees' self-esteem. When employees have a balanced and healthy sense of who they are, they are less susceptible to burnout. Lerner (1989) provides five guidelines to aid people in establishing and maintaining a balanced sense of self.

The first suggestion is to present a "balanced picture of both our strengths and our vulnerabilities" (p. 35). When we are able to do this, we are not easily influenced by what others say or think about us. We know that although we have weaknesses, our strengths by far outweigh them. This is essential in a functional workplace, but it becomes even more important when there are dysfunctional executives, managers, or fellow employees.

The second recommendation is to "make clear statements of our beliefs, values, and priorities, and then keep our behavior congruent with these" (p. 35). This can be a more difficult task. We have learned that our beliefs and values developed and were integrated into our personalities early in life. In fact, it was assumed that we would incorporate our parents' beliefs and values. In reality, the healthy family system teaches young people to explore family beliefs and value systems and then incorporate those that will serve them well. Another part of the myth of establishing beliefs and values early in life is that as we continue to mature, these can change. It is possible to reconsider old beliefs and decisions based on our greater experience. If we hold too rigidly to untenable beliefs and values, we can become rebellious. Rather than accepting those that are beneficial to us while rejecting those that are not, we tend to disregard all of them. This can lead to serious consequences. We all need a code by which to live. If we abandon all of our previously held beliefs and values, we are like a ship without a rudder.

Lerner suggests we "stay emotionally connected to significant others even when things get pretty intense" (p. 35). If we follow this observation, we can learn how to respond to stressful situations without losing our sense of self. Some family systems' and organizations' responses to difficulty are to deny, avoid, or distance, all of which tend to intensify the problem rather than move toward a solution. When we stay emotionally connected, we learn to accept other people as they are. We avoid trying to make them just like us. We also learn there are many ways to approach and solve problems. Ours is not the only or the best way.

The fourth recommendation is to "address difficult and painful issues and take a position on matters important to us" (p. 35). Coping by avoiding painful issues, whether in the workplace or within the family, can contribute to long-term difficulties. The adage "no pain, no gain" is an accurate assessment of what happens during a period of growth. At the very least, advertising and some television programs suggest very strongly that happiness is the ultimate goal. We are told that we can have everything we want as long as we are willing to work for it. Family systems and the work force can also promote this concept. The harsh reality is that people hardly ever get everything they want. Life is a series of trade-offs. Sometimes life is tough, difficult, and unfair. Others can run roughshod over us, trampling on our value systems and beliefs. We can experience a job loss, divorce, children who don't measure up to our standards. Often it is through no fault of our own that painful issues arise. If we can identify and address them, we are on the way to coming to terms with them. We will not resolve all of them. Life is messy at times, and there are times when we have to take a position on something. Not to do so would challenge our integrity. This may even mean losing a job, a spouse, children, or friends. If we are able to clarify our values and beliefs, we can more readily meet this challenge when it arises.

Lerner's final recommendation is to "state our differences and allow others to do the same" (p. 35). We are not all going to agree. Each of us has our own set of values and beliefs that guide our life. Not all people think alike. This does not mean that some people are wrong and some are right. As human beings, we are entitled to state what we believe, as are others. If people are mature, they can accept differences. Mid-life people have experienced many situations. Most have worked either outside the home in paid positions or as volunteers. Others have run households and raised children. Some have done both. It is ridiculous to think that when these people arrive at the workplace, they become little children. They bring a good deal of knowledge and expertise with them, and employers who encourage their workers to use these in the workplace will experience a more productive and perhaps innovative work force.

Burnout does not get better by ignoring it. It begins slowly, grows over time, and appears suddenly. When these flare-ups happen, we can be sure that they were in the works for some time. The early stages go by unnoticed because many of the people who burn out are competent, self-sufficient men and women who compensate for their weaknesses.

Employees' Guide to Recognizing Burnout

Periodic checks can help us identify possible burnout. Freudenberger and Richelson (1980), in their classic work on burnout, list questions people can ask themselves. I present their questions below, but I have added my own examples and comments.

Do you tire more easily? Feel fatigued rather than energetic? A quick look at one's work schedule can provide valuable information. If the time spent working has not increased, look at the load. If this also has not changed, examine the relationships at work or within the family.

Are people annoying you by saying, "You don't look so good lately"? Listen to their comments. Often others see things before we do. Check your eating habits. Listen to what your body is telling you. If you are able to eliminate a possible illness, then you may be becoming burned out.

Are you working harder and harder and accomplishing less and less? Perhaps the organization is dysfunctional. You were excited about your current position. You began working for the organization, then found that the organization's external philosophical agenda is different from your operational agenda. This could easily lead to burnout as you try to come to terms with the cognitive dissonance that is happening.

Are you increasingly cynical and disenchanted? Again, you may have bought into the promise of things to come. As you continue to produce, you find that you are not rewarded. Others receive raises and promotions while you receive a pittance or are passed over. When you talk with your employers about the situation, they give you mixed messages.

Donald was promised a promotion. He later learned that David was to receive the promotion. When Donald confronted his boss, he was told that David was willing to give up everything for the company. David wined and dined clients, provided women, and kept the clients happy. Donald's beliefs and value systems made this type of involvement impossible. Maintaining a close relationship with his family is very important to Donald. As a result, he was not available at a moment's notice day or night, which his boss used as a reason for passing him over for promotions and raises.

When people begin to experience burnout, they may be overcome with a sense of sadness. Oftentimes they cannot identify the causes. Companies who create situations where workers have a purpose will find increased productivity and a sense of peace and contentment within the workplace. Feelings of sadness undermine an employee's ability to handle a job effectively.

Marsha, a very productive team player, is falling behind on her work. She does not seem to have any enthusiasm. No one is able to cheer her. One of her colleagues comes to you for advice. He describes her behavior and indicates that people are beginning to notice. He has tried to talk with her, but she is unreceptive. In looking over Marsha's files, you discover that she has not received an annual interview, which is customary for all employees in that division. One of the long-term goals listed on Marsha's initial interview was to increase her salary and status within five years of her employment, which has happened as planned until this year. In discussing the matter with her manager, you discover that the division hired a new employee in a parallel position to Marsha's. This person received a starting salary equivalent to Marsha's current salary, and Marsha has been responsible for training the new person. Marsha's response to this situation was a sense of sadness. She felt that she had not reached her personal goal. Rather than ask for input on the new employee, Marsha assumed she was entirely responsible for her inability to receive an increase in pay or a promotion. People suffering from burnout do not talk over the situation with their supervisor or the human resource specialist. Instead, they take the entire responsibility for the situation.

Are you forgetting appointments and deadlines? Preoccupation often is the culprit; thus, it becomes necessary to identify what is causing the preoccupation. Increased stress detracts from day-to-day happenings. Time and energy are spent trying to equalize the stress and maintain a sense of balance. Everyone experiences this occasionally. If this continues over time, productivity will suffer.

Are you increasingly irritable? More short-tempered? More disappointed in the people around you? People either attempt to rescue or stay away from those who are difficult to approach. This leads to isolation and perhaps some paranoia.

Josh has always been respected for his easygoing approach to life. Recently, he has isolated himself from others. When questioned, he replies that he would rather by off by himself than snap at people, and he figures it will all blow over. Your records show that coworkers began noticing changes over a year ago. It is no longer a temporary state of mind. Asking Josh for his appraisal of the situation could provide an opportunity to explore the situation. If there are other symptoms of burnout, Josh needs to address this problem. If he does not, Josh could find himself not only without friends and supportive coworkers but without a job as well.

Are you seeing close friends and family less frequently? This leads to isolation. The burned-out person finds it more comfortable to spend more time alone. This is counterproductive because people who are burning out need to interact with others. They can more readily increase their self-awareness when they hear what changes others perceive.

Are you suffering from physical complaints like aches, pains, headaches, a lingering cold? Often this is a sign of high levels of stress. Our bodies begin telling us to slow down. If we do not heed the warnings, our bodies slow us down.

Are you unable to laugh at a joke about yourself or tell a joke about yourself? Laughter is one of the great healers. When we can laugh at ourselves, we relieve internal tension and stress.

Do you have very little to say to people? As burnout progresses, we become more preoccupied with ourselves. We find we have little in common with others. Again, we find a predisposition toward isolation.

As you go through the various questions, you can make some determinations for yourself. The more often you respond positively to these questions, the more likely you are as a candidate for burnout. You must take inventory of yourself before you begin to identify others who you think are experiencing burnout. Your burnout may be affecting others within your organization. If you find that you are doing fine, then you can use these questions as a basis of conversation with employees who seek your help. Burnout is not something you can take care of for others. This information will help you understand the process of burnout. When you recognize potential burnout, you should refer potential victims to competent providers who can help.

Organizations need to take the whole employee into account and provide a positive atmosphere that encourages employees. The result could be a work force that devotes its energies to attaining the company's goals. There is one difference between this company and the company that wants to own the employee. In this healthy, concerned organization, employees work their jobs. When they leave, they have time and energy to attend to their other responsibilities.

Take a Look at the Organization

If you are confronted by several employees exhibiting possible burnout, here are some questions you can ask to determine whether the organization is the cause.

Are there departments or sections that lack clarity regarding the organization's goals and objectives? You will probably need to look at the organization from the top down to determine where the breakdown occurs.

Do the units within the organization promote each other? It is possible that an unhealthy competitiveness has arisen between the units or between the managers of the units. The employees may feel caught.

When directives or instructions are given, are they direct enough so that employees understand what they mean? Do employees know how to respond to the directives? Are the tasks clearly defined? Are they too rigid, thereby taking initiative from those employees who are responsible? Where applicable, can employees make plans to participate in continued skill building and increase their competency? Does the organization change quickly or slowly enough to allow employees to adapt to the changes? Are employees sufficiently informed of potential changes? Are they informed when expected changes do not occur?

Does the organization provide help for employees who do burn out? Is the organization receptive to them on their return if they need a period of time away from the job?

LAYOFFS AND TERMINATIONS

Layoffs and terminations happen in all organizations, but responses in a dysfunctional organization differ form those in a healthy organization. All employees within a unit respond to these events, whether they are personally involved or not. If the organization is dysfunctional, they will probably attempt to diminish the importance of the layoffs or terminations. They may even seek support from those employees who remain, which could lead to confusing behavior on the part of the remaining employees. A major change in a unit within the workplace represents a loss, evoking certain normal responses. Employees who remain may actually feel relief that they were able to continue, possibly followed by feelings of guilt, grief, or fear.

The Process That Accompanies Layoffs and Terminations

There can be a group process that accompanies layoffs and terminations. It is important to remember that processes take time. It is also valuable to know that people have feelings about events that happen around them. Society in general and perhaps the organization as well do not always provide a safe setting for people to work through their feelings. What is involved in this process? First, there may be denial that the event is occurring. The person involved and coworkers alike may become involved in the denial process.

Second, people may begin to experience health problems. These are normal responses to excessive stress. As long as people are in denial, these health problems may be there. Units within the organization may notice high absenteeism and lethargy. Employees may complain of their inability to sleep or of wanting to sleep too much. They may also display symptoms of not caring. This is a result of the emptiness that people feel when major changes occur.

Once the initial stages have passed, people may display emotional outbursts. They may become angry or hostile. As they begin to process what is happening, their feelings may become confused. They feel relieved that they still have their jobs, but they also feel empathy for the people who were terminated.

Some people also go through a stage of wanting to leave the organization. They want to quit to make up for the unfair treatment received by their friends and coworkers. The stress and tension levels tend to increase during this stage of the process.

Eventually, people begin to disengage from those who were terminated. As this happens, there is a move toward a sense of equilibrium. Finally, those who remain employed return to their normal emotional functioning. This can be a bumpy ride for the corporate structure as well as for management if not prepared for these normal responses. Grief is part of the loss process. People grieve over their own losses and those of others. This is especially true when there is closeness because of friendship or proximity.

WAYS TO ADDRESS CHANGE

Organizations experience internal changes because of the changes that are taking place throughout the world. Those organizations that operate from a dysfunctional mode will find it difficult to make the move to a more open system of operation. Even those organizations that are willing and able to address change rapidly will find it disruptive at times. One of the ways both of these types of organizations can improve their chances of success is through continual learning within the organization. The concept of learning cultures gives companies a place to start. Since this concept promotes the notion that companies form their own particular style, it is a flexible process to use.

LEARNING CULTURES WITHIN ORGANIZATIONS

Times are changing. The total organization is recognized as important, starting with the top executive and including the lowest-paid employee. With companies facing more competition, they need new operational modes. Changes are an everyday occurrence, but can be threatening to everyone involved. Those who hold power positions will learn how to use change to their advantage. They can promote and live by a message of the positive advantages of change. It is important to communicate this to all employees.

Information gathering is essential. With the huge amounts of data available, it is an art to use that information without overwhelming people. We need to use new techniques to absorb vast amounts of information, find the nuggets helpful to the organization, and proceed from there.

Top executives and managers will find it helpful to create agendas that serve their purpose. This means narrowing the scope and concentrating on those areas identified as most important. When managers spread themselves too thin, they lose their ability to be direct and specific. As a result, they send mixed or confusing messages to their employees.

The tide is turning. The competitive world of today demands economic and moral responses. Power as it was known and used is no longer respected. The new managers of today and tomorrow are focused, informed, thoughtful, and disciplined.

How does a business move from the parlor games of yesterday to the straightforward, disciplined style of the management of tomorrow? This is a difficult question. We are dealing with a multifaceted problem. Change does not work unless there is a major commitment from the very top. The older we are, the more difficult it is to make major changes in our behavior.

A second aspect of the problem is that workers are accustomed to certain management styles. These may not be in the best interest of the workers, but they have become institutionalized. The more levels there are within an organization, the longer it will take to persuade all employees to make the changes.

A third difficulty is that change involves a process. Processes take time. Employees may even welcome the changes presented, but they may not be able to respond immediately. They prefer the comfort that comes with the known to the fears involved with the unknown. Since the majority of the work force is quickly becoming middle-aged, specific issues need to be addressed. First, organizations are faced with long-term mid-life employees. Then there are those who are changing careers and are new to a particular organization. Reentry employees are different from the long-termers. New mid-life employees, including women and minorities, are another group. Each group will have different types of issues relating to work force issues and changes.

Today we recognize learning as a lifelong pursuit. Adapting to today's rapid changes depends on people's ability to plan for and recognize when change is happening. Today's changes also involve more than the United States and exhibit a global direction. This learning is no longer about how to do the job better, faster, or more efficiently. It is about how to deal with diverse cultural differences. Organizations themselves are different. One type of learning is interacting with the variety of styles and responses to the needs of the nineties. A second is interacting with other countries' organizations.

Schools and universities prepare young people to fill positions, but it is not uncommon to hear how unprepared these young people are to respond to the organization's needs. These educational institutions seem to do a better job of passing along already rote information. They do not fare as well when asked to produce students who are willing to ask questions, probe, and try different ways of doing something. Mid-life people who return to institutions of higher learning often find themselves involved in myriads of work, little of which has much to do with their everyday life. They take notes, memorize, and give back to instructors what is expected.

It is important to have a liberal education. Knowing where we've been helps us to create a better future. Along with that knowledge, we need to learn new and different ways of approaching problems, working with groups of people, and responding to the common good.

Jaccaci (1989) has given some thought to expanding the notion of the social architecture of a learning culture. He suggests that we need to move beyond developing organizational cultures. If organizations are to succeed, they will need to design learning cultures that incorporate the entire world. He describes a learning culture as "one where collaborative creativity in all contexts, relationships, and experiences is a basic purpose of the culture. ... The whole culture learns in a self-aware, self-reflective, and creative way" (p. 50).

To establish this type of learning culture, a human resource specialist needs to be well informed. Unprecedented changes will occur. Attitudes and behaviors that served people well in the past will no longer be adequate. Considerable and constant change will rule the day. Each and every employee will need to learn new ways of doing things. Although each employee will benefit over the long haul, the short term can be harrowing for all involved.

Today information, services, and relationships are at the heart of organizations. The old models of obedience are no longer effective. New questions will be asked. According to Jaccaci (1989), those questions will include, "What is our organization's life purpose, and why?" Unless everyone within the organization can respond to these questions, there will be problems.

Galagan (1989) has developed a learning map based on Jaccaci's concept of a learning culture. The whole concept will not be presented here, but several ideas that flow from the map will be discussed. For a better appreciation of the total concept, you are encouraged to read Galagan's "Growth: Mapping Its Patterns and Periods."

The map Galagan presents is a way of looking at the four-stage evolutionary process involved in human learning. The first stage, labeled "gathering," is the formative stage. The same kinds of units increase in size by gathering resources to themselves. The second stage is "repeating," which is the normative stage. Similar units reproduce themselves. It is the stage of more and more but not different. The third stage is "integrating," in which you bring differences together to create something bigger than the sum of its parts. Galagan suggests that this is the stage of high creativity. It is necessary to let go of the previous stage in order to operationalize this stage. The fourth stage is "transforming." This stage allows the creation of a higher-order entity. Jaccaci calls this stage the "Age of Ideal Intention," which follows the information stage. He suggests that human learning is about to move to what he calls the transformational level. This is a move from doing to being.

For this type of movement to occur, there needs to be a cadre of people dedicated to informing others. They can establish methods and systems to teach how to achieve the transformational level. Mid-life people would be a valuable resource, since one of their developmental tasks is to create. Erikson's (1950) generativity versus stagnation stage happens during the later part of mid-life. Part of this stage is the recognition of a need to leave a legacy. Another part is the increased importance of relationships. Relationships are what the current information society is all about. This becomes apparent as more is written about the individual within an organization. Meeting people's needs within the work force creates a less stressful situation. One result is that people can better handle family stresses.

People with different talents are identified. Each plays a role and contributes to the whole. The first is the trainer. This person shows others how to do something for a specific purpose. Then there is the educator, who enables people to use what they already know, and gives people the opportunity to use that knowledge within a broader context.

The next is the mentor, who helps others to identify their talents and capabilities. The mentor can add another dimension by helping people to clarify why they do what they do.

The visionary continually reminds everyone that our ultimate goal is the good of the whole. The prophet, the last type, is the one who asks the tough questions: "Who owns life?" "What is the universe about that there should be life in it?"

When organizations begin to care about people, people will respond in a positive manner. But a huge learning process needs to take place before this happens. Human resource specialists are about people. They provide the connection between the individual on the front line and that person's manager. One of the major tasks needed to be done to set this new learning concept in motion is to teach people problem-solving skills. Let people solve the problems that they discover. Too often, we step in. We have the answers and we know exactly what needs to be done. With a little patience, we can ask the right questions so that people solve their own problems, including problems within the workplace. People become dependent. Dependence is especially fostered when people have used their own problem-solving skills only to have the solution discredited by someone higher in the pecking order. After a while, people choose to ask rather than spend the time and energy only to find they are in error.

Possible Changes in Training Workers

Mid-life workers have worked in a traditional work force. According to current information, major changes are making their interactive skills obsolete. Even mid-life people who are entering the work force for the first time or are reentering after a time out of the work force will probably expect traditional behavior.

Organizations, facing stiff competition from competitors, are using the team approach to capitalize on the brain power and skills of their employees. The team approach is popular. It addresses the issues of innovation and commitment. All aspects of the organization are called on to work together rather than to continue the competitive spirit so popular during the 1970s and 1980s. A major problem that most organizations face is the traditional mode of their structure. There is a heavy top-down communication style. Management is used to controlling situations and workers. The question becomes, "How do traditional organizations turn the 180 degrees necessary to become team oriented?"

Teaching team-building skills is an obvious answer. According to Huszczo (1990), this is an appropriate move. He foresees problems because typical training programs are not necessarily structured to incorporate the team approach needed for the 1990s. He points out several issues that trainers need to know to be successful.

The first mistake that trainers make is to overlook the distinction between team building and teamwork. Previously, organizations used team building and teamwork to help people feel good about themselves and others. They concentrated on building relationships within the organization. Team building covers more than this particular outcome. There is more freedom involved. People are encouraged to gain the skills needed to work together to achieve the goals of the organization. Teamwork has often been ineffective as far as accomplishing the tasks it set for itself.

Throughout the literature on organizations, a key word is *open*. Teams, to be effective, need to understand their relationship toward the total organization. In a closed system, the organization assumes that people will work for it. In an open system, the organization must reward team effort. The team concept is altered when individuals within the team receive rewards because people again begin to work for their own benefit. Individuals become less important within a team atmosphere, but if the team functions at its best, the total organization benefits.

The team members must know their individual strengths and weaknesses. Part of the team approach is to combine different learning styles, personalities, and operational styles together to form the team. The assessment of the team members is essential to training a team more effectively. Trainers need to develop individual assessment measures that reflect the goals of the organization and the employees. It is human nature to want to follow a predetermined tool like a recipe. Every trainer knows this. Often trainers find themselves called to task because they did not give specific instructions to take care of any problem.

There are problems inherent in assessment. Assessment requires open and honest discussion about weaknesses within the team. Collecting data, an important part of the process, also can cause conflict. Workers who are insecure or have problems may feel threatened. Only team members can change or solve the problems the team is having. This requires a high level of problem-solving skills, Though it may be painful at first, teams that work openly and honestly toward solving their problems will be more effective.

Team members need to practice team skills together. Sending a team member for training with the hope that the person will bring back information for the whole team to use doesn't work. If it is impossible for an entire team to attend training, then strategies need to be worked out so that the individual can share the information. There needs to be a commitment to team development.

Using the team approach does not mean that every team is going to look and function alike. A team needs to fit the goals of the particular organization or workplace. Teams made up of employees who have been with the organization for a long time will need input different from that needed by teams that have a number of new employees. According to Huszczo, "Teams need training and strategies to capitalize on their unique talents, personalities, organizational situations, and task assignments" (1990, p. 40). Because of the time it takes to train team members, some trainers will want to develop a model to use for every team within an organization. Obviously, if we accept the premise that every team is somewhat different, this is not a wise decision. There are times when the team approach seems to have failed. Before rejecting this concept, check the structure of the training model used with the team. If packaged training was used, then it could be the package that failed and not the team approach.

People can learn to work in teams. The real test is actually functioning as a team. Trial and error is a far better instructor. The team must use the knowledge and skills taught. Continual learning is inherent in this approach. When teams notice a specific weakness, they should have the flexibility to draft other members to fill the weak spots.

Teams are responsible for the knowledge and skills they learned in training. Their work should reflect increased competency. This is an ongoing process, and again accountability is essential. Rewards play an important part as well. Remember, this is a drastic change from the emphasis on the individual.

HUMAN RESOURCE SPECIALISTS' ROLE

It is wise to remember that typical mid-life employees have reached a point in their lives where certain outcomes are important. First, they are dealing with their sense of who they are. They are also evaluating their lives. This is the time in their lives when they reestablish their dream. They begin to integrate their work and family lives for a better balance. They may no longer want to climb the ladder of success but want to broaden out. They begin to establish different goals. They often feel that they have paid their dues. If they cannot be the president of the organization, they want at least to have some say over their lives within the work environment. Often, except for reentry workers, they have proven themselves; now they want to make a difference. If what they want does not fit what the organization wants, there is conflict. If the organization doesn't care about the personal goals and lives of its mid-life employees, it jeopardizes itself. Let's take some time to look at the organization. In doing so, we can perhaps identify ways in which the organization can profit from its mid-life employees. We will also look at ways in which the organization can be its own worst enemy.

Major Outcomes Expected by the Organization

Basically, organizations exist and are successful only to the extent that they meet their objectives. In our economy, the major objective of an organization is profit. There are two main resources within an organization: its capital and its human resources. Actually, the human resources are the key to a profitable and long-lived organization.

To achieve maximum output from human resources, organizations must develop their programs so that they are at a competitive advantage. Most of the time, organizations devote energy and money to accomplishing designated activities because activities are more easily monitored and evaluated. You, the human resource specialist, can be buried under paperwork. You are responding to activities like hiring, compensation, EEO compliance, and performance appraisals. All of this is important but often takes on a life of its own. Remember, it is within your scope of responsibilities to provide a service that helps the organization meet its ultimate objective, profit.

Traditionally, the way human resource specialists aided in the profit agenda was to minimize the cost of human resources. In this model, emphasis is on reducing turnover, dealing with legal compliance, reducing health care costs, deemphasizing labor disputes, and minimizing absenteeism. All of these activities can be measured quite easily.

Areas that are more difficult to measure involve getting more output from investment made in employees. This calls for another approach and probably different administrative practices. Since the payoff is more long term than short term, selling this idea can be difficult.

There are some basic issues involved. The organization must embrace the idea of looking at innovative ways in which to succeed. Everyone in a decision-making capacity needs strong commitment to the process. Hiring practices need to be in line with the organization's philosophy; for instance, jobs should be tailored to fit the personnel hired. People succeed where they utilize their talents. As progress outdates current knowledge and skills, employees need to be retrained. Nothing succeeds like success. The important advice in this adage is to tell people when they are doing a good to outstanding job. Positive input pays by promoting more positive output.

What are some ways to achieve this positive approach to human resources? First, when people find their jobs meaningful, they respond more positively. They are willing to work because they enjoy what they are doing. Most mid-life people spend a good part of their time at the workplace.

The human resource specialist needs to be aware of the organization's needs. The specialist must have the skills necessary to aide the organization's adaptation to more profitable ways of utilizing its workers. Both the organization and the employees win.

One way to begin this transition to addressing a more competitive advantage is to look at human resources as investments rather than expenditures. Employee turnover, office space, hiring, and training cost money. It is no secret that employee costs have risen over the years. When the firm hires a new employee, what is the long-term investment on the part of the organization? A rule of thumb that has been used for years is that a new employee costs the organization money for the first six months on the job. After that, the employee has the potential of being an asset to the company. By the time people reach their middle years, they have some positive assets. They know what they are doing. They have a backlog of experience that serves them well in continued training. They do not waste the company's time, energy, and money. Since they have already been successful, they don't worry about whether they can learn new information or skills. This is the optimum scenario. On the other hand, some mid-life workers are as insecure as the newest, youngest worker hired.

Invest in additional human resources only when you can expect a reasonable return. Remember, when you hire someone for a particular position, you may be hiring the person for life. Even if the employee leaves, the position remains to be filled again and again.

Consider alternative kinds of employment. Hire temporary help at peak periods rather than increasing the full-time staff. When hiring new people, be sure they are the best for the job. Also, it is helpful to know that they have as few lingering problems as possible. Hiring a middle-aged man who has recently been divorced or widowed may take some additional resources. The person may be the best qualified for the position, but personal problems often affect the workplace. You could choose not to hire the person, but a more workable solution would be to hire him and then direct him to the various support groups your organization has to offer. Pretending there isn't a problem or discounting the problem won't make it go away. Addressing it head-on and providing support may help to resolve the problem. This can promote good public relations and a sense of loyalty on the part of the new hire.

Although you are not a counselor by training, you are involved with people. You have a responsibility to know when the people you are working with need more or different kinds of help and support. To use your time and energy effectively, you need to be creative in responding to the organization and its workers. You are a catalyst, a planner, and a problem solver. You can be an effective liaison between employer and employees. If you become too involved in situations and with people outside of your area of expertise, you too can burn out. Utilize all the resources you can muster to maintain your perspective and provide the kinds of support services for which you were hired. Let others within or outside the organization provide the support groups and counseling necessary.

6

Managers' Dilemmas

What they didn't teach, what they taught and you forgot, what they didn't know to teach and you need.

Unless you are a recent graduate, you probably were not exposed to the new realities of organizations. The most significant is working within a global economy. As other countries maximize their work forces and become more competitive, the United States is forced to do so as well. To be competitive with the more expansive economy takes a different approach to product and employee.

You may have learned this during your formal education, but when you began working you found another set of realities. The organization in which you began work followed the more traditional model. You were to keep the assembly lines moving. People were second to product. The bare minimum needed to keep people content and producing was used. If employees became too much of a problem, causing a lag in production, they were terminated. Today, this is no longer acceptable behavior. Employees recognize that they have rights as well as responsibilities. They also live more complex lives; change is not only part of their work experience but part of their personal lives as well.

Some of the major issues facing human resource specialists are the rapid changes occurring with the work force, especially on the management levels. The differences between younger workers and mid-life workers have an impact on worker satisfaction. Discrimination is still a concern. Racism, ageism, and sexism in the workplace affect productivity, loyalty to the organization, and workers' sense of themselves.

RAPID CHANGE WITHIN ORGANIZATIONS

American companies are in the midst of a revolution. Competition has been the backbone of the American economy. During the 1980s, maintaining a competitive edge became more and more difficult. Previously, companies that incorporated a new technique along with a better product knew they would corner the market for a long period of time. Now change happens too quickly for any organization to rest on its laurels. Peters (1987) suggests that eighteen months is becoming a normal time span for occupying the leadership position.

Mid-life people are experiencing this rapid change in their personal lives as well. They are finding themselves in better health, more able to keep highly productive, and wanting to have a larger share of input in their own work life.

You are in a position to provide mid-life workers with the encouragement and support they need to continue to be effective workers. Whether this is an easy or difficult task rests on the philosophy of the organization for which you work. Is it moving toward a shared employee-employer job situation? If so, then the organization will expect that you have some ideas and plans to aid in bringing the work force along. If not, then your job is made more difficult. Mid-life people are choosing to look at other options. One of their developmental tasks during this period in their lives is to assess their involvement in their work. Not all will be free to make the changes that they would like to make. Those who can may leave. Some of those who can't will decide whether to adjust their attitude and move along with the company. Others will continue to work but will find their sense of fulfillment outside the workplace. Needless to say, the latter group will not perform to company standards.

LEADERSHIP VERSUS MANAGEMENT

It is not uncommon for organizations to either ignore or totally accept different approaches when they are trying to keep a competitive edge. Recently, much has been made of the importance of leadership. Leaders are being touted as the most important ingredient in restructuring organizations. As a result, managers are falling into disrepute. Those companies that ignore the need to add a broad array of leaders will fall short of their goals. This is also true of companies that disregard managers and put the total emphasis on hiring and developing leaders.

Task Differentiation

Tasks for leaders and for managers are different. As a result, there is a normal tension between leaders and managers. Organizations that continue to operate out of an "either or" mode will not take advantage of this natural tension. They will not be able to recognize the myriad of possibilities that come from an "and also" approach.

According to Hickman (1990), managers represent the "analytical, structured, controlled, deliberate, and orderly" (p. 7). Leaders tend to be involved in the "more experimental, visionary, flexible, uncontrolled, and creative" aspects. Managers implement policy. Typically the manager is the person involved in the day-to-day operation. Leaders represent the spirit of the organization. They are more interested in the future. Both are absolutely necessary within organizations. In the real world, people can possess characteristics of both leadership and management. Depending on the task, they may use either their leadership or their management skills.

Those who are primarily in leadership positions tend to seek opportunities, have vision, identify problems, look at the organization as a partnership, and come up with broad, sweeping generalizations. The manager will see the pitfalls of change, attempt to visualize the impact of change on the day-to-day operations, provide solutions to the problems identified. They may view the organization in a more hierarchical manner. They move incrementally. Each step is put in place before the next step is tackled.

Corrine and Walt share the responsibilities of the human resource area in an organization. Corrine was hired five years ago based on her ability to see a large picture. She is very creative and can rattle off three or four scenarios with little thought. Walt has been with the company for twenty years. He has been very effective in solving day-to-day issues that arise within the organization. Everyone likes him. People within the corporate structure as well as subordinates can approach him in an informal manner about their concerns.

The organization decided to make a major change to become more competitive. This was the result of many meetings and informal conversations with managers and subordinates. Walt was informed that the new goals would require additional retraining and the hiring of different types of people. Because Walt was secure in his position and over the years was able to recognize his strengths and weaknesses, he suggested that the organization hire another person to work with him. After further discussion, it was decided that the other person should be complementary to Walt and not a clone. As a result, Corrine was hired.

Over the years Corrine and Walt worked together. They identified their strengths and agreed to disagree, but each was able to compromise so that the company's goals were always met. When Walt became too rigid in his thinking and approach, Corrine would initiate a meeting. Through respectful dialogue, Walt would ease up and try different ways of achieving the objectives set forth. The same was true when Corrine's creativity exceeded the capabilities of the organization. The two have capitalized on the tension between leadership and management. Those subordinates who are particularly creative seek out Corrine when they want to share their ideas. Corrine helps the employees cultivate their ideas and serves as their advocate in implementing the changes that result. When the day-to-day operations bog down, employees go to Walt. He is able to deal very effectively with employees who require more stability and need more time to integrate change. Problems still exist. Mistakes are made, but the company is close to reaching its goal of being recognized as a first-class competitor.

Style Differences between Leaders and Managers

Because of the differences in operating styles between leaders and managers, great care will need to be taken to provide ways for each to understand the other. Typical leadership-driven organizations seem totally unstructured and flexible, whereas management-driven organizations are far more structured and disciplined. Attempting to meld the two so that each can operate successfully is difficult.

Organizations headed by leaders will be spontaneous, unstructured, and process oriented. Those headed by managers will follow the status quo more frequently, will tend to add more structure as change is integrated into the organization, and perhaps will become even more formalized. The human resource specialist can provide assistance in bringing the two types together for more effective use of both styles. You can easily tell which type of person you are dealing with by the individual's response to change. The manager might say, "Ours is not to reason why." The leader, on the other hand, will want to know why something is being done and is interested in doing only what's worth doing. Each can stifle the organization. In the spirit of good faith, the manager may begin to question everything until no one is able to get the work accomplished. On the other hand, the leader may begin to question how things will be done to the exasperation of all involved. It becomes important for you to be or to identify an expert in communication skills who can work with both groups together to point out when they have reached a point of diminishing returns.

This becomes difficult because the two groups process differently. Managers tend to think in a straight line. We often call this logical thinking. Leaders think laterally; they zigzag through, move in what seems to be unconnected patterns. Sometimes they arrive at the same conclusions as the logical thinkers. Other times they arrive at surprisingly fresh, workable solutions. It is difficult for people to appreciate the opposite way of thinking. This probably causes more problems among individuals, groups of people, and organizations. If teams can be established in which each type of thinker is respected and appreciated, then the two can work together. As a result, each makes a contribution to the whole. New ideas are formulated and then presented in a logical, systematic way.

Another difference is the way each type approaches people, situations, and problems. Leaders prefer to confront, hit the issue head-on, clarify where everybody stands, get things on the table. The manager is prone to want to smooth things over, avoid confrontation, and avoid any disruption that can result from confrontation.

The leader needs to learn when to confront, and how much, whereas the manager needs to evaluate what smoothing things over will do in the long run. Again, if each is working with the other, the two can help each other decide. Getting people to do their homework and to learn why they are doing what they are proposing aids the organization. Once that skill is learned, people find that it serves them well. There are times when it is wise to step back and let people have time and room. Leaders might follow the top-drawer strategy. Present the idea. If there is no interest and absolutely no response, put it in the top drawer. Try again later. Nothing stays the same. The timing could be off. As you can see, because of the different ways managers and leaders think and act, an enormous amount of tension may be created. The trick is to use that tension as an asset. Consumers, employees, management, the corporate structure, and the business or corporation will all benefit.

Leaders versus Managers

Today, there is talk about the differences between managers and leaders. In traditional organizations of the past, it was taken for granted that the person who headed the organization was the leader. Those who carried out the day-to-day activities were the managers. The emphasis was on producing. Employees did whatever they were told. That style of leadership and management emphasized the outcome more than the competition did. Little attention was paid to employees' needs. Companies now have begun to realize that without their employees, they have nothing. They are more aware of the interplay between work and personal life and that both need attending. One of the ways to seek a better balance is to look at leadership and management styles within the workplace.

Hickman (1990) identifies the natural tensions that exist between managers and leaders. Stability, authority, duplication, and instruction characterize managers. Thriving in crisis situations, influencing, originating, and inspiring are the ways in which leaders function. This tension is not necessarily bad, but when the tension becomes intrusive and animosity rules, problems can grow out of proportion. There are times when each style is appropriate; the two together can promote a stronger, healthier work force. For instance, workers should recognize that managers tend toward uniformity and that leaders seek unity. Programs, policies, control, and consistency are important to a manager, whereas people, leading by example, empowerment, and commitment are important to the leader.

The two types respond to external and internal change differently as well. Managers like stability and compromise. They will react, plan, reorganize, and refine. In times of change, leaders will seek out crisis, will polarize so that events and situations are looked at differently. They are proactive, looking to the future rather than dealing with the present. They prefer to experiment with a variety of ideas rather than set down a plan of action. They rethink rather than reorganize. They are more prone to revolutionize. It is not too difficult to see how each type has something to offer. Neither by itself is effective in the long run. The manager reigns in the leader, and the leader prods the manager.

Another area where this is evident is evaluating performance. Managers are more interested in performance and in providing compensation. They are conservative in business dealings and are interested in the short term, the present. Leaders look for potential. They want to increase the satisfaction level of employees. Risk taking is important. Leaders are future oriented. What is best for the long term? Again, companies that employ and value both styles are better equipped to meet the present and the future.

Leaders may be hired in management positions. They then reflect a different type or style of management. On the other hand, managers may be identified in leadership positions. If the organization identifies the traditional roles of management regardless of the style the person brings to the job, there will be problems. Again, if you know the strengths and weaknesses of management and leadership styles and have encouraged the organization to hire both, you may also find yourself involved in preparing the organization for differences in operating style. This may involve offering training sessions, educating employers and employees on what to expect, or providing sessions and information on team building.

During the 1970s and 1980s, many management positions were cut. True, there were too many managers. Companies were top heavy. When people had achieved a certain numbers of years of employment, had accomplished a positive record with the organization, or had proved dismally ineffective, they were promoted to management positions. In fact, promotion was the major payback to the loyal employee. There were few other options. If people were not promoted, society looked askance at those individuals. With a different view of leadership and management, people will no longer be promoted as frequently based on the old traditional model.

When there is a better balance between the goals of the organization and employee involvement in attaining those goals, fewer people will be promoted to management positions because there will be fewer management positions. Only those that are needed for the entire organization to work at its best level will be available. This will not cause great concern for employees because there will be other ways in which their work is rewarded. The main way will be in greater involvement in their own work and a better understanding of how it fits the total picture. There can be a problem group of employees, though.

Employees in Traditional Organizations

Mid-life long-term employees have worked most of their lives in traditional organizations. Often they still measure their success by the old standards. The managers who were rifted in the 1970s and 1980s were middle-aged people. They had come to believe the myth of the good old American dream. If they did what they were supposed to, made money for the company, and put the needs of the organization ahead of their own, they would be rewarded. Some had the opportunity of a buyout and so were not financially strapped. They could begin to search the labor market if they wanted.

On the average, mid-life people who become unemployed spend a longer period of time searching for other employment. Some become discouraged and change their status from unemployed to retired. Many continue to look for the same type of employment that they held in the past. Others realize that retraining or learning a new area of expertise is necessary. Despite predictions that people would change careers three or more times during their working life, mid-life people did not think this applied to them. Others were glad for the chance to do something else. They were in jobs that they didn't necessarily like, but they had been in them for most of their working life. To leave them voluntarily was too great a risk.

Mack had begun working for a company when he was twenty-two years of age. He was married and had a child. Over the next ten years, he and his wife had three more children. Mack was promoted several times. By the age of thirty eight he reached the top of the ladder. By the time Mack was forty-five, he had begun to tire of the work he was doing. He felt burned out. He dreamed of starting his own business. He wanted to run a bookstore, but he kept his dream to himself. He had three children in college, and his wife had returned to finish her undergraduate degree. Mack and his wife had purchased a new home several years before. Although it was their dream home, they also were feeling the financial squeeze of monthly payments. Mack put aside his dream of a bookstore. He continued to work and tried to change his attitude. When Mack was forty-eight, the company was sold. The agreement was that all the present employees would continue. Although Mack experienced feelings of doubt, he continued with the company. Within two years, the company reorganized. Mack was told that his position was being eliminated. He could be transferred to another state and take a position there with a considerable decrease in pay, or he could seek other employment.

Mack's decision rests on a number of issues. Suppose that Mack has only one child left in college. His wife has graduated and obtained a management position that pays well. Mack is convinced that he does want to explore the bookstore option. He negotiates and leaves with three months' more pay than originally offered.

On the other hand, suppose that Mack has two children in college and a five-year-old. His wife has chosen to stay at home and raise this last child as she did the others. They are considering selling their dream home and buying something smaller. Mack has been looking for a comparable position with another organization. He knows that the bookstore is a dream that probably won't be fulfilled.

A third scenario is that Mack does nothing. When the consolidation happens, Mack is moved within the new organization. He takes a third cut in pay, and his position is not secure.

At any juncture within each of these examples, the human resource specialist can be helpful to Mack. Support services available within the community can help Mack make the best decision possible at the time. You may even have an outplacement service within the organization or may have contracted with an outside firm to do this for you. Mack may not ask for help. He may not even realize that it is available. Organizations that promote and provide these services can profit in the long run. Changes do happen within organizations. There are people who do not fit the new organizational thrust. Working with these employees rather than leaving them on their own can have long-term benefits for the organization.

Reorganization

Subordinates find themselves in similar circumstances when companies reorganize. These people may have more problems with finances and other employment. Mid-life people who are semi- or unskilled workers may find that the only type of employment available has a low pay scale. Although there are retraining services available, these people may be at a disadvantage. Some do not have the capability of being retrained. They were able to do the job they had because they learned it early in life and perfected their ability over the years. These people would be classified as unemployable. Others could respond to retraining but either are not aware of the service or cannot get past the sense of failure a job loss signals to them. Still others may have health problems that keep them from participating in retraining. Even if they completed the retraining, they may be unemployable because of their health.

Those mid-life people who are older have been choosing to retire early. Part of this is because of their individual financial situations. Many are more financially secure than in the past. Companies are also offering packages that they cannot refuse. Part of the reason is their inability to adjust to the rapid changes occurring. Also, those who were adventuresome and were willing to take risks to change their job or the work force found that they were not rewarded. The sense of failure that incurs has also encouraged people to leave the work force while they are still considered middle-aged. Another type of manager or subordinate is the widowed woman. If the woman was employed before her husband's death, she will probably be able to continue to work. She will have an income. If she has a standard of living that requires two wage earners, she will either have to make major adjustments or lower her standard of living. If there are children in college or other unmet financial commitments, she could find herself in dire straits.

If the woman was not employed before her husband's death, she may need to seek employment. Although she has skills and abilities resulting from raising a family and keeping a home, many times these do not transfer easily to the job market. Also, her age may work against her. There will be certain areas of employment not available to her. She also may not have the reserve funding necessary to explore self-employment or small-business opportunities. Often, middle-aged women are excellent prospects over the long term. But it takes a good deal of foresight to take the risks involved in hiring them.

YOUNGER WORKERS VERSUS MID-LIFE WORKERS

The work force is changing rapidly. Young workers have been educated and trained differently. The values they hold are different from those of their mid-life counterparts. They also cost companies less in wages, since they are just beginning. Middle-aged workers who have been in the work force for the greater part of their working life have almost reached the peak of their earning power. The organization has already invested a great deal in these workers. Replacing them with younger workers may be cost-effective in the short term, but it is important to look at the long-term costs. Can middle-aged workers be retrained so that they do not become obsolete? Is this more cost-productive? Obviously, organizations currently disregard the effectiveness of this process. Many mid-life people are, for the first time in their careers, finding themselves seeking employment.

Some companies choose to continue to employ mid-life workers but do not invest in them. The workers either are too close to retirement or are not judged capable of being retrained. These workers may easily lose their enthusiasm and begin marking time until the day they retire. They may have learned a passive response to their work. This may be so ingrained that it is impossible to get them to change their way of thinking about their work or to become involved in retraining. This passive response is not entirely the fault of the employee. According to how organizations functioned in the past, employees were to do their jobs and were not encouraged to get involved in a personal way.

People learn early whether they can make mistakes and experience failures without keeping the mistakes hidden. Innovations do not come without risk and mistakes. This is the path to a more perfect product or service. Keeping errors or mistakes secret precludes fixing whatever it is that is less than perfect. Covering up can lead organizations into serious trouble.

DISCRIMINATION AT THE WORKPLACE

The changes that are happening within corporations could give the mid-life person an advantage, a second wind. Chaos, constant change, and the search for the competitive edge are all part of today's work force. Because of previous conditioning, mid-life workers may find this particularly difficult. You play a sensitive as well as a tough role. Cutting through the issues that impede production while maintaining highly motivated employees is no easy task. Couple this with the ageism, racism, and sexism that exist within the work environment and you may ask, "Why didn't they tell me about the complexities facing human resource specialists?"

Racism

Downs (1971) provides an operational definition: "Racism may be viewed as any attitude, action or institutional structure which subordinates a person or group because of his or their color." He goes on to explain that racism is more than just attitudes. Actions and institutional structures can also be included. He defines an institutional structure as "any well-established, habitual, or widely accepted pattern of action or organizational arrangement, whether formal or informal" (p. 77). Racism occurs when subordination is the result of attitudes and actions. Both overt racism and indirect institutional subordination because of color can exist in the workplace. It is the latter that is more subtle. There are times when being aware of one's color, or taking that into account when making decisions, is not necessarily racist. The key component, according to Downs, is *subordination.*

Gary's company has several openings. He traditionally does not advertise but relies on word of mouth. Past employees and his friends are aware of the job openings. There are no minorities currently employed, nor have there been minority workers in the past. The chance of minority workers learning about these openings is minimal. Therefore, they are excluded from employment in this company. This is not overt racism, but it is an example of indirect institutional subordination. This practice may be benign. The owner has not reviewed his hiring practices, and as a result, groups do not have equal opportunity to apply for the jobs available. He may not even be aware that his oversight has indirect racist effects.

Wellman (1977) argues that the basis for continued discrimination is the scarcity of resources. Although more minorities now are employed and may even have management and professional types of employment, the power and control are still held by the white majority. According to the U.S. Census Bureau (1985), year-round full-time earnings for 1985 showed that black men earned 69.7 percent and Hispanic men 68.0 percent of the earnings of the white male. Gill (1989), in his study on discrimination and occupational structure, found that employment discrimination is partly responsible for racial differences in occupations including professional, managerial, sales and clerical, and the crafts. An outcome of this finding is the economical impact on the black wage earner.

Ageism

Another source of discrimination affecting the workplace is ageism. Ageism is acting on the negative stereotypes that continue to exist based on people's age. According to Butler and Lewis (1982), ageism involves prejudicial attitudes, discriminatory practices, and institutional policies and practices. Age bias can affect individuals because others may react to gray hair and appearance, attitudes, and behaviors. Thus far, when people begin to exhibit outward signs of aging, they and others regard them as no longer useful. As more people live to seventy-five years and beyond, these stereotypes could vanish. One way this can be hastened is to continue to incorporate the later middle-aged and older person into the work force.

Ageism: A Mid-Life Issue

One normally does not think of ageism occurring during later middle age. However, the discrimination that middle-aged people experience within the job market can be defined as ageist.

Age discrimination is a structural barrier to occupational development that involves denying people promotions based solely on age. The federal Age Discrimination in Employment Act is intended to promote the employment of workers between the ages of forty and seventy based on their ability rather than their hire. It is unlawful for employers to refuse to hire or to discharge workers solely on the basis of age. It is also unlawful to segregate or classify workers.

Age discrimination occurs in several ways. Employers can make certain types of physical or mental performance a job requirement and argue that older workers are thus incapable. They can make cuts in the number of employees in an attempt to get rid of older workers by offering attractive buy-out plans. Snyder and Barrett (1988) reviewed approximately six hundred federal court cases filed since 1970. The employers were favored abut 65 percent of the time. Job performance information was the key factor. Most of the time, this information was presented using the differences between young and old workers. The courts, for the most part, did not question the inaccurate information or stereotypical views presented by the employers.

Keeping Mid-Life People Involved

Besides the experience and wisdom that can be gained through involvement in the work force over a considerable amount of time, mid-life workers have other contributions they can make. If they are looked on as competent and respected for their years in the work force, they could more likely become an asset instead of a liability. It takes time to train young people. It takes life experience to make judgments that withstand the test of time. Older middle-aged people, like adult learners, learn through analogy. They compare the current situation or problem with others they have experienced. They can spot pitfalls and avoid making rash moves based on the crisis of the moment. Younger people do not have the backlog of experience from which to bounce off new ideas, plans, and behaviors. In time, they too will have the life experience necessary to avoid rash or too quickly made decisions.

The median age of the work force is rising. As already noted, the majority of workers will soon be middle-aged. This covers a broad range, from about forty-five through about sixty years of age. There are differences among the various ages included, but for the most part, this age group will be healthier and more active than their cohorts even ten years ago. They will probably live longer, with more stamina and more drive. Education has not been wasted on this group. For the most part they will be better educated, be curious, and will have continued to learn. They will want to continue to make contributions to society. For a number of years now, middle-aged workers have been encouraged to leave the job market through layoffs, displacements, and buy-out plans. They have been leaving as they are nearing their peak.

Rather than losing this valuable resource, organizations would profit more by providing time off so that these workers can recreate and retrain. Rather than making these workers obsolete by discouraging retraining and updating skills, companies could encourage them to seek new avenues for their talents.

The labor shortage that is evident today in some sectors will continue to grow and will incorporate other areas. The workplace will need to find new ways of recruiting, training, and managing middle-aged workers. Mid-life workers want a sense of autonomy in their lives. They have reached middle age. They have paid their dues. They want to interact to a greater degree. they have knowledge and life experience, which can prove to be a rich source of information for organizations. Human resource specialists may even see the day in the not-too-distant future when, rather than devising plans to disengage the older middle-aged worker, they are called on to restructure benefits packages. These packages will need to address the needs and expectations of the work force and provide incentives to reduce job turnover. They may even be structured to encourage older middle-aged workers to retire later rather than earlier.

Sexism

A third source of discrimination in the workplace is sexism. Sexism is defined as any act that directly relates to a person's gender. This is different from sexual harassment, which may also be present.

Baron and Bielby (1985) found that sex discrimination is pervasive and is sustained by diverse organizational structures and processes. This segregation drastically restricts women's career opportunities by blocking access to internal labor markets. DiPrete and Soule (1988) found the greatest disadvantage facing women occurs near the boundary between lower-tier and upper-tier grades. Women move to the top of the lower tier and remain there. Men are typically promoted to the upper tier. Pay discrimination is also alive and well. Traditionally, women were paid less because men had families to support whereas women were supported by husbands. Those women who were not—single working women—did not need as much income because they did not have a family to support.

Although statutes have been passed to prohibit discrimination in the workplace, real change won't happen without fundamental changes in social attitudes. No real changes will occur until we believe that men and women should be provided equal opportunities for all occupations. Everyone should be paid based on the kind of work done rather than on gender.

As a society, Americans are obsessed with sex. Sex threatens to overtake the preoccupation with money because it generates an enormous commitment of time, thoughts, and energies. Sex is treated like a thing that can be quantified, evaluated, and avidly consumed. There is a good deal of competition involved as well. Sexual freedom, which was heralded as a solution to repressed sexual activity, has not curbed the desires, appetites, or enactment. When taken to the furthest conclusion, sex can be very disruptive.

Sexual Cultures within Organizations. Every organization has a sexual culture. Whether this culture was developed through conscious decisions or whether it evolved, it does exist. White (1986) identifies several ways people can determine what the culture is in a particular organization. The first is the language. What of a sexual nature is freely discussed? How? The words that are used to communicate about sexuality reveal the values and attitudes. The type of sexual humor and the way it is used provide more insights into this culture.

Artifacts also reflect the sexual culture of the organization. Physical objects like paintings, sculptures, photography, books, and magazines project an image of the organization.

Ethics and values are another way of determining the sexual culture. Are the values of human relationships clearly defined? Does an ethical code of behavior exist for the employer, employees, and clients? Are there formal or informal rules regarding sexual relationships among employer, employees, and clients? What is the picture the organization presents to its clients about sexual relationships?

The final area is relationships. How is affection expressed physically and verbally? Is there sexual gaming and harassment within the workplace?

Not infrequently, what is proposed to be the attitude of the employer toward sex within the work environment is not enforced. There are at least two reasons for this. The first is that although employers talk about and issue policies that reflect a harassment-free workplace, they do not follow their own guidelines. Second, they may follow their policies but turn a blind eye when others within the organization do not. In either case, the disharmony that is created can cause havoc within the organization.

Mid-life workers are not immune. In fact, part of the reevaluation of one's life includes sexuality. Some middle-aged men who realize that they are growing older turn to sex to prove their youthfulness. This is condoned within the society and even encouraged through the double standard. Men become more attractive as they grow older while women become less so. It is okay for men to pursue extramarital escapades. We all know that boys will be boys. Men can't help it. It's in the genes. Our advertising promotes goods through the use of sex. Young beautiful women present the products. There is still present a persisting and deep-seated sexism. Social subordination and sexual objectification of women are part of the depersonalized, commercialized, and coercive sexuality found in society today. Women are still relatively less powerful than men and thus less economically secure. A system that continues to provide women with fewer employment options and less pay keeps women dependent on men. The continued male dominance in our society mitigates against any major punishment involving sexism or sexual harassment.

Moral and Political Issues

Sex issues are both moral and political issues. Some organizations continue to have women "available" for their clients. They view this as a good way to secure business in a competitive marketplace. Males within the organization still meet periodically somewhere else to mix business and pleasure. Some of the pleasure involves having women available. Some of you reading this are saying: "Wait a minute. This is 1990. That no longer happens." Dan, twenty-five years old, recently announced that he would need to find other employment. The company for which he works provided a week away from the work environment for some of its employees. Wives were to join the men in the middle of the week. For the first two days, the company provided women for the men. When the wives arrived, the work began. This young man refused to participate. He is looking for another position for two reasons. He does not subscribe to this type of behavior. He knows that eventually he will have to leave. Though there are women who work in this organization, they are employed in traditional, low-paying positions.

Sexual Harassment. A clear-cut definition and description of sexual harassment is lacking. This has caused problems for people attempting to establish a code of behavior or misbehavior. It also makes it difficult to determine the extent to which sexual harassment does occur. Usually when people talk about this subject, they are referring to the sexual cooperation that is gained by promises of rewards or threats of punishment. A second interpretation of the term is sexist and/or sexually offensive behavior without the implication of required sexual exchange. F. J. Till (cited in Fitzgerald and Hesson-McInnis, 1989) conducted a study using a national sample of college women. His goal was to determine if there were general items that were reported by each of the women involved. Five categories were identified. The first was gender harassment, which included generalized sexist remarks and behaviors not necessarily directed toward sexual involvement. The remarks involved insulting, degrading, or sexist attitudes about women. The second was seductive behavior, which was not tied to any sanctions if cooperation was denied. This included inappropriate and offensive behaviors. Sexual bribery, the third type, involved promises of rewards for sexual activity. Threat, the fourth type identified, involved coercion of sexual activity by threats of punishment. The fifth, sexual imposition, was the actual use of sex, often through assault. Till, through a factor analysis, found three levels of harassment: (1) gender harassment, (2) sexual coercion, and (3) sexual harassment. He suggested that these were levels because of the increase of intensity between each type. Problems of definition and description remain, but this provides a basic understanding from which to address harassment issues.

Another problem worthy of mention is that the first level is the more difficult to substantiate. Gender harassment lies in the eye of the receiver. Some women refuse to integrate gender-harassing remarks. Their sense of self is such that they pass off remarks that are made. Other women take offense at general or specifically degrading comments about women.

The Equal Employment Opportunity Commission (EEOC) has defined sexual harassment as follows:

Unwelcome sexual advances, requests for sexual favors, and other verbal or physical conduct of a sexual nature constitute sexual harassment, when (1) submission to such conduct is made either explicitly or implicitly a term or condition of an individual's employment; (2) submission to or rejection of such conduct by an individual is used as a basis for employment decisions affecting the individual; or (3) such conduct has the purpose or effect of unreasonably interfering with an individual's work performance or creating an intimidating, hostile or offensive working environment (Woods & Flynn, 1989, p. 46).

Sexual harassment includes requests for sexual favors in return for job benefits, leering, intentional touching and patting, salacious gestures and other advances that invite sexual activity, and other verbal and physical abuse. The EEOC requires that the "workplace be free from sexual harassment and intimidation" and that employers take a "firm, proactive role in the prevention of sexual harassment in the workplace" (Woods & Flynn, 1989, pp. 45–46).

Another ramification is the element of sex discrimination. The Supreme Court in 1986 ruled that sexual harassment constitutes illegal sex discrimination. Woods and Flynn (1989) also felt that the Court needed to define the liability of the employer.

Legal controls are a step to eliminating sexual harassment, but if workers are to be free from sexual intimidation and exploitation, there need to be changes in the way women are perceived. Historically, women were seen as the property of men, satisfying men's needs and taking care of their homes and families.

Sexual Harassment in the Work Force Is a Prevailing Concern for Human Resource Specialists. Unwelcome advances or requests for sexual favors is unlawful. In spite of this, the behavior persists within the work force. A survey of U.S. Merit Systems Protection Board (Kandel, 1988) indicated that 42 percent of women workers said they had been sexually harassed between 1985 and 1987, which equaled the number reported in a similar survey seven years earlier. The types of harassment were somewhat different, however.

More prominent today is the hassling type of harassment. Supervisor harassment puts the employer more at risk than coworker harassment. In the latter, employers are liable if they were aware of the harassment but failed to take prompt and effective remedial action. Harassment cases are difficult to judge because there are usually only two persons involved, the offended and the offending parties. Third parties, which include relatives, friends, coworkers, and advocates for the harassed, tend to increase the emotional pitch of the ordeal.

Sexual affairs between managers and their subordinates can be demoralizing for the supervised unit because of the couple's on-the-job conduct or because other employees perceive favoritism and lack of confidentiality. The affair that goes sour leaves the employer to pick up the pieces.

One of the major problems identified by mid-life women reentering the work force is the lack of respect paid them by their male counterparts. They are unprepared to handle the comments and sexual innuendos. Mid-life women who change from more feminine types of professions, like elementary and secondary teaching, to the corporate world also feel unprepared for the attitudes of the men with whom they now work. It should come as no surprise to you that with the increase of women in the work force there is also an increase in sexual harassment. Woods and Flynn (1989), using figures from the Bureau of National Affairs, estimate that 40 percent of women are sexually harassed at work. Sexual harassment results in financial and emotional cost to the victim and to the company. It also takes its toll on the workplace. For these reasons, the company needs to establish a sound sexual harassment policy.

It becomes the responsibility of the employer to make sure employees at all levels in the organization understand that sexual harassment can produce individual liability for related offenses. Those offenses include intentional infliction of emotional distress, negligent infliction of emotional distress, interference with employment, invasion of privacy, solicitation for prostitution, assault, battery, and rape. Employees need to be reminded that even routine occurrences that some people find offensive, such as remarks, looks, pictures, pats, and touches, are the sources of most harassment suits. Third parties who are not subject to sexually based conduct can raise claims of sex discrimination. They can base their claims on the fact that although they have been excluded from sexually charged behavior, they find it harassing to work in an environment where others are approached or are a party to this type of behavior.

For a sexual harassment policy to be effective, it is important that an effective and well-publicized disciplinary system be in place. Employers need to stress severe sanctions for violators. Communication must be clear and repeated often. The policy needs to be implemented in a firm and evenhanded manner.

If sexual harassment is the outcome of attitudes toward women, then laws and employer compliance can diminish the extent to which it occurs. A more difficult problem facing us is when the perpetrator is a sex addict. Two major characteristics of an addict are denial and the need for a fix to a sense of self. Therefore, policies and disciplinary actions will not be effective with addicts. Treatment is the only effective means for them to stop perpetrating their addiction.

Maureen, a forty-nine-year-old widow with two children in college, was offered a job by an old friend of her husband's. Maureen was thrilled. She felt she was competent for the position, and she had some fresh new ideas that she thought would enhance the organization. About two months after Maureen was hired, another person was hired to work with her. Maureen was told the work load had increased and that she needed more help. Maureen spent three weeks training the new person. When Maureen received her evaluation, she found that her performance was considered above average. Six months later Maureen was told that the new employee was going to be promoted. Maureen would then be working for the person she had trained. When she asked for an explanation, she was told confidentially that she was the better person but was not as flashy. The department head needed to improve his image. One of the ways he decided would help would be to have a younger, more attractive person meeting the public. Maureen began to watch more carefully. She noticed that the newer employee was often in conference with the department head. They ate lunch together several days a week and worked late as well. When Maureen asked others with whom she worked about the situation, she found that they suspected the new employee was using her looks and charm to get ahead. When Maureen asked the new employee about her interactions with the department head, she was told that the woman was doing whatever she had to so that she could move up within the organization. When Maureen approached the man who arranged for her job, he suggested that Maureen needed to have a little fun on the side. She was becoming too serious and intense. He suggested that she accompany him on a business trip the next week. They could talk over the situation and try to come to some closure on it. Maureen's long-term absence from the work force had left her naive and unable to deal with the situation.

Sexual Addiction. Sexual addiction is a problem that can be related to sexual harassment and sexism in the work environment. Some of the identifying characteristics of a sex addict are a repeated history of one-night stands, abortive love affairs, or broken marriages. Sex addicts include those who are chronically polygamous or unfaithful. Men may at times dream of being a Don Juan; some may have tried to fulfill that dream. Sex addicts are the few that actually live this life-style with ease, determination, and success. This does not imply that they are happy or contented. Often they suffer a great deal and continue to use their addiction in an attempt to make themselves feel better, only to continue to feel insecure. They have a poor sense of self, which is enhanced when they are attacking out of their addiction but which fades again when the high is over.

This addiction, like others, cannot be cured by prayer. It is not a simple moral failure or a bad habit. It is a compulsive disorder that overrides moral restraints. Sex addicts compromise their own ethical standards, their loyalty to their spouses or partners, their concern for their own reputation. Guilt is an overriding emotional response for most. Some, however, have no feelings of remorse and may also be suffering from borderline personality disorders.

Work, family, friends, and social lives are compromised. People who suffer from this addiction are often willing to sacrifice their jobs and careers. They construct their lives around their compulsion. Those who choose to act out their addiction in the workplace cause disruption, which can lead to low morale. Because there are work environments that subscribe to the mandates about sexual harassment in word only, sex addicts can continue to perpetrate their addiction. Companies that enforce a strong policy against sexual harassment may drive sex addicts to act out their behaviors in other sectors of society.

Importance of Reporting. In the literature on sexual harassment, people are advised to check out all reported incidents: Where there is smoke, there may be fire. This is true in the case of sex addicts as well. Since you are not a trained counselor, what can you do when you suspect you have a problem with a sex addict? Part of the answer depends on how you arrived at your suspicion. Have you been approached by a family member? This is possible in organizations that provide support services for employees and their families. Directing the spouse to an employee assistance program is the first step. Working with the employee assistant to observe behaviors could provide the information necessary to confront the addict. Confrontation is important, but to do it successfully, there has to be reason and proof. You may not be able to obtain these without seriously invading the employee's privacy. The best option may be to introduce the spouse to the people who can help.

Families suffer the consequences of sex addiction. Spouses and children can be caught up in the lies and denials to the point that family life is chaotic. This affects them outside the home as well. Spouses may find it difficult to be productive on the job and may even display unhealthy behavior. They may not even know what is causing their inappropriate responses at work. Those who do know the cause cover up for their spouses out of a false sense of loyalty, fear, or their own pride.

Children could become involved in acting-out behavior, which disrupts the family even more. Getting to the cause of the problem can be difficult because many people use triangles to focus elsewhere. They become involved in apparent problems that take their attention away from the cause of the real problem. Children can become the focus of attention. There are times when both of the spouses know that the child is not the cause of the problem. They promise each other that once the child's behavior is handled, they will address the issues that caused this behavior in the child. Often, once the child is settled, the spouses forget their promise. The sex addict seeks a fix, and the spouse responds negatively or secretively. Children begin to react again. Unless there is a major external intervention, this behavior continues.

Friendships can be abandoned to hide the problem. Those friendships that continue for the sex addict encourage the addiction. There is a veil of secrecy surrounding the family. From the outside, the family may look like the ideal family, but no one ever gets close enough to see what is really happening. If a wife shares some of her concerns with friends, the husband can easily sluff it off. "You know how women are. They are so possessive and read evil in every action." Or in the reverse case: "My husband has been under a lot of pressure lately. He is even accusing me of being unfaithful." Because addicts are master con artists, people easily believe their explanations. It takes an astute person to catch the clues.

Another way in which sex addicts can be brought to your attention is through other employees. One or more may come to you. The stories they tell may seem so far removed from reality that you may question whether they are telling the truth. Early detection and referral can save you and the company time, energy, and money.

Types of Sex Addicts. In the following section, characteristics of the various types of male sex addicts identified by Trachtenberg (1988), along with a brief scenario of how they might relate within a work environment, will be presented.

The first type is the "hitter." These men deliberately seek out sex. Often any woman will do. The fix comes in the pursuance and the act. Once the act is completed, hitters disengage. They spend a great of time finding their next partner. They are always on the lookout.

The hitter is the person within the organization who has made advancements toward most of the women. He may even slight his job in order to pursue the woman of his choice. Usually everyone knows about this person. His reputation precedes him. When hitting on women in the workplace becomes too dangerous, he escapes to the community at large. This man is usually single. He is incapable of making any type of commitment. These are the type that women think they can change. These women delude themselves into thinking that if this man met the right woman, he would settle down. Once everyone knows about him in the workplace, he moves outside the work environment. The damage has been done in terms of the emotional and psychological distress he has caused the women.

"Drifters" are another type. These men find women everywhere. They do not use much time and energy seeking them out. They like to keep their options open. This means that they want to continue seeing other women. This man projects self-assurance, is charming, and is very persuasive. He approaches sex in an easygoing manner. He is willing to wait, to have a couple of dates before becoming sexually intimate. He has a very strict set of criteria that kick in once he is intimate with a woman. He finds fault with all women, but he really does believe that he will find the right woman, given enough time.

These men do not treat women as sexual objects. They tend to see them more as social assets. Their misleading charm is that they feel little need to spend much time with their current lovers. They are not jealous or possessive. But as the interest wanes, the drifter begins to feel angry toward the woman and moves on. Usually the woman does not know why the relationship has ended. Drifters tend to be single as well. They are the men everyone says the single woman should meet. They are often described as a great catch.

The workplace is a convenient place to meet many women. Because the drifter continues to see the woman for several months at least, he does not have the same reputation as the hitter. In fact, the woman may feel she is inadequate and is the reason the relationship ended. What becomes difficult in the workplace is that the drifter forgets the woman very quickly. This could cause stress, tension, and anger.

The third type are the "romantics." These are at first glance the most appealing. They are passionate lovers, but sex is not the reason for their involvements. Their fix comes in the guise of total emotional involvement, to the exclusion of any outside interference. They dream of a relationship without anger, tension, or boredom. When any of these traits show themselves, romantics are disillusioned. They leave the relationship broken-hearted and angry. They feel that have been used and then abandoned.

The "nesters" want companionship as well as romance and sexual excitement. They ask for commitment, but once the marriage or housekeeping is set up, they withdraw. They are the type who go out for a pack of cigarettes and never return. They are often basically lonely men who want the closeness they remember or imagine from childhood. They move too quickly into a commitment and then find that it is lacking. They unconsciously see women as a potential entrapment. They will choose avoidance over confrontation, causing them to walk away from commitments when problems arise.

"Jugglers" seem to maintain long-term relationships but are not monogamous. They are always involved with at least two women at a time. In fact, they do not act in secrecy. Each of the women involved knows about the other. These men need to be in control and fear attachment. This type gives off mixed messages, which women deal with for a time. Eventually, the partner chooses to no longer put up with the ambivalence and leaves. The relationship crumbles under the weight of the demands placed by the juggler. This is the type who is walked out on most often.

"Tomcats" are a paradox. They are obviously unfaithful but at the same time devoted to wife and family. They do not want to change their home situation, but they also want the freedom to have affairs. They are the more pronounced version of the hitter, drifter, or romantic. These are the type that people talk about, make comments about, and perhaps even envy. They may even choose women who have a low need for sexual involvement. They interact in a filial way with their wives. This also allows them to have an excuse for themselves and their mistresses about why they need to seek sexual fulfillment outside the marriage. There is a hopelessness that comes over the marriage and a sense of helplessness as well. The wife continues to believe that the tomcat will change, but the husband cannot change. At other times, the wife denies his behavior and continues to act as though they have a perfect marriage. Both become trapped.

This is just a smattering of the information available on sex addicts. It is not sufficient to give you the ability to identify specific individual types. It is presented here because sex addiction, like any addiction, needs to be treated. Some of the behavior of each of the types described above will infringe on the sex addict's behavior in the workplace. Or the spouse or the person involved with the sex addict may exhibit behavior that is not conducive to the goals of the organization.

It will probably be because of other behaviors that these people will come to your attention. You will be in a position to refer them to experts to deal with their problems. You may become privy to information about their cases. If you are aware of sex addiction in general, you will at least know what EAP people or other experts are talking about. You may also be asked to cooperate with a recovery program. The program will make more sense to you and you will be able to do your part if you know something about sex addiction.

SOME DILEMMAS THAT HUMAN RESOURCE SPECIALISTS MAY EXPERIENCE

Not all employers or employees deliberately violate the various "isms," that is, sexism, ageism, and racism. Sometimes, practices have been part of an organization throughout its history. Less attention was paid to claims and accusations before the 1970s. People were often dealt with quietly. Sometimes violators were allowed to stay because of the influence they had within the organization, with competitors, or within the community.

Since organizations are attempting to respond to global competition as well as to increased pressures within the United States, they cannot afford to ignore employees who implicate them in lengthy lawsuits following inappropriate behavior. It will often fall to you, the human resource specialist, to address these problems.

You will also be expected to understand management and leadership roles. You will be in a position to develop and present models as well as training so that upper management becomes adept at identifying those who work from a manager's perspective and those who possess the traits of a leader. When employers and upper management are clear about their roles and how they work out of these roles, employees will find it easier to work within the organization.

If your company espouses the dignity of all workers, you will be able to apply creative and innovative approaches while aiding the organization in meetings its goals. This may involve retraining, continuous learning, and changes of attitudes and behavior. You are a pivotal person as change continues to nudge and encourage organizations to change accordingly.

7

Technology's Impact on the Workplace

In this chapter several areas of particular interest to mid-life workers will be discussed. Among these are the ways in which technological advances affect mid-life people. This includes obsolescence, retraining, and lateral moves. The value and place of continuous, lifelong learning in general and how it relates to this particular age group will be explored. The ins and outs of early retirement and its impact on mid-life workers as well as on the work force and the workplace will be discussed. This chapter will also include a general overview of changing careers as mid-life option or task. The final section will look at the role of the human resource specialist in light of the various topics presented.

TECHNOLOGICAL ADVANCES

Why the commotion about competition? Basically, it has come about because of the shift from a manufacturing and industrial economy to an information- and knowledge-based goods and services economy. Additionally, the pressure of a global perspective puts more pressure on organizations and their work force. The changes and advances in technology affect transportation and communication, which in turn contributes to a high level of mobility.

These new technologies contribute to new businesses, which provide a great deal of competition for existing businesses and services. Some of the latter find themselves obsolete and fail. Others fight the obsolescence and attempt to keep up with new businesses and services.

The baby boomers and the increased number of women in the work force have caused a shift in values. Workers are looking beyond the paycheck.

They want to achieve self-fulfillment and satisfaction with their lives in general and within the work environment. Time has become a precious commodity for the dual-career families. Work has to provide a quality of life, a sense of well-being, and high levels of commitment to make it worth the time away from children and family. People are beginning to recognize and work for a sense of dignity within the workplace.

Necessary Restructuring

Until recently, the United States was a leader in technological and educational achievement. It was considered one of the most prosperous nations. This is no longer the case. Other countries are catching up and at times surpassing the United States.

American corporations are finding that because of the global competition they are being forced to restructure. They need to reevaluate their recruiting, hiring, firing, and management policies. Coates, Jarratt, and Mahaffie (1989) in their article, "Workplace Management 2000," identify seven themes they say describe the emerging work force. Most of the themes either have been mentioned before or will be mentioned later in this chapter. They bear repeating. The first theme regards the ability of the work force to adapt while the management is less rigid and more flexible. As the entry-level labor pool decreases, other potential workers will be sought, including the handicapped, underemployed, retirees, women, and minorities. Traditional management styles will need to be altered to work effectively with these groups.

A second theme recognizes that home life and work life are not mutually exclusive nor separate entities. Dual-career families, the shift to the home as a workplace, and the emphasis on an information-based work force change management styles and accountability. All too often we think of people working at home because of day-care problems and the desire to be with small children. Mid-life people who have teenage children are also choosing to work at home. With the increased potential of teens at risk, some parents would rather be at home during the hours their teens are not in school. This emphasizes the need for flextime as well.

A third theme is globalization, which includes the integration of world economies. Although this has been looked on as a major factor forcing changes within organizations, it can be seen as very positive as well. During the transition process, workers and corporate managers could experience new or different types of stress. Once organizations learn to work more cooperatively and are able to move past the takeovers and negative competition, more positive benefits could accrue. Workers will need to learn to view work from a different perspective. Actually, in time there may even be a major shift toward an exchange of workers among countries.

This will take some reeducation and retraining. This first became apparent during the 1970s when many industrial jobs were lost because of changing technology. Many workers waited for their jobs to return. They refused either to retrain or to relocate. In fact, politicians continued to promise the return of jobs, especially within the auto industry. Those who were not involved in the auto industry knew that wasn't possible. But the displaced workers held on to the dream of returning to their previous jobs long after it was no longer feasible.

Everyone with any influence on workers needs to be in concert about the changes brought about by modern technology. Time, energy, and money were wasted in the 1970s to the detriment of the country as a whole. All would have been better served if those who were in charge could have admitted the situation as it really was. The second outcome of these major layoffs was that people chose to retire rather than relocate. Americans, especially blue-collar workers, are used to staying put rather than moving to another state. This long tradition will need to change as we move more fully into a global economy.

The fourth theme of the emerging work force suggests that human resource planning occurs in conjunction with business unit planning, not separately. Human resource personnel will play a broader role than in the past. They will provide a better interface between workers and the work they are to accomplish within the goals and parameters of the organization. This means that human resource people will need to know more about the company, its goals, desired outcomes, and any major changes anticipated by the organization. A movement toward meeting the competitive forces can cause major upheavals within the work force. Human resource people will need to be in tune with all the possible reactions that might occur within the work force. They will also be responsible for working with employees as the latter move through the various transitions.

Another important theme of the emerging work force explains the changing technology and operations at work. These changes make continuous training and education critical, if not mandatory. Enhancement of skills becomes even more important within an information-based economy. Insufficient numbers of workers have the necessary tools and skills. Therefore, considerable retraining and education will be necessary. A basic outcome of an information-based society is that many jobs that will be available and must be filled are highly specialized but low paying. Technological advances will replace people performing the same types of activities. Workers will need to develop new skills in order to function along with these technological advances.

It will be necessary for organizations to balance the employees' demand for benefits with the cost to the corporation. Until recently, workers could depend on widely based health insurance coverage at little or no cost to themselves. Today, they are being asked to pay more out of pocket for less coverage. Companies can no longer afford the high cost of health insurance for their employees. Organizations are offering incentives to workers to cut the cost of health care. Innovative measures need to be taken to ensure that workers have the coverage they need at an affordable cost to employee or employer.

Corporations are being pressured to redefine their responsibility regarding social issues. Some of the areas they are being called on to examine are the role they can play in reducing the trade deficit. They are being asked to aid in changing the declining quality of education, to respond positively in fighting the problems of drug abuse, and to work toward reducing environmental pollution, to mention a few.

This is happening at a time when organizations are also facing a number of problems related to their own needs as they attempt to become a viable part of the global economy. If they ignore the issues that society designates as important to the well-being of the country, they may find a good deal of opposition as they attempt to put in place the changes they deem necessary for their survival.

The New Look and Actions of Corporations

Peters (1987) presents several characteristics the successful firm of the 1990s and beyond will have. First, it will be "flatter." There will be fewer layers within the organizational structure. This could prove to be troublesome for mid-life workers. Their picture of having made it within their occupation or job could easily rest on how far they have been promoted. This is not entirely without reason.

Traditionally, the mark of success for the worker has been advancement to a management level. This is true for white- and blue-collar workers. Doing away with this type of advancement can prove to be difficult. It will be necessary to aid people in rethinking the concept of success. Using a team approach with rewards or incentives can be effective if proper education is given the workers. It is essential that when the term *team approach* is used, it is truly meant. Oftentimes organizations use the current buzzwords but fail to implement the concept behind them. Changing titles or names of things does not necessarily mean that anything different will happen. For instance, it is popular now to use the term *multipurpose room* instead of *conference room*. Does anything different happen as a result? Is the term *multipurpose room* more descriptive of what happens in that room? When a person stops to think for a moment, *conference room* depicts a serious, work-oriented concept. *Multipurpose room* suggests a looser, more playful scene. Is this an effective change? Which concept does an organization wish to convey?

The second characteristic is to have more autonomous units. There isn't someone off in an office somewhere making decisions; the experts are as close to the product or service as possible. To have this autonomy effectively in place, employees needs to be trusted to know what they are doing and to have the company's interest at heart. Companies that rule from afar have reason to be concerned. For every level of authority between the product and the creator, there is a loss of ownership. Communication also becomes garbled and is often misunderstood or lost completely. It is difficult to maintain a high degree of pride and interest when the employees are only following directions.

More emphasis on quality is long overdue and needs to be explored. One of the major objections about American-made goods is a perceived lack of quality. To keep abreast of the competition within the United States and globally, organizations need their products and services to pass the consumer test of quality. Quality is difficult to achieve if employees think that the company is only out to make money. If they perceive that they have little value or worth as individuals, they will not be committed. The result is less than quality goods and services.

Again, a team approach could help insure quality. When a group of people are involved in a particular mission, they can provide input, encouragement, and a sense of pride. It is surprising that so many Americans gripe about the poor quality they receive for the money they pay. Yet they continue to produce poor quality. It is almost as though it is someone else's problem. Americans feel that they deserve quality but do not have to produce it. This too will take some reeducation. The onus of accountability lies with everyone within the organization, from the "top dog" to the "lowliest employee."

Service is another characteristic that becomes even more necessary. One aspect involves the service providers within an organization. These are the support staff, who are absolutely necessary if products or services are to be forthcoming. It is essential that people who are hired in support services recognize that their job is to provide the service gladly and willingly. When a particular group or person needs media support to make a presentation, then it is the job of that group to provide the best support possible. Often, support service people can use their particular talent or expertise to get back at others whom they perceived have done them wrong. This is not professional and is detrimental to the whole organization. There should be other means by which these kinds of wrongs can be addressed.

A second aspect of service involves the consumer. Recently there has been an increased awareness and more time and energy spent by companies who espouse the motto, "The customer is always right." It is important that action follow. Lip service to this motto doesn't work. It doesn't help when customers file a complaint and receive the service they request, but begrudgingly so. Goodwill and a positive image are very important to organizations. They need to have people who are able to convey a sense of professional competency whenever or wherever necessary.

Organizations of the 1990s will need to be more responsive, not reactive. They will have to risk and be proactive to keep abreast of the competition. This means making mistakes at times. If people within an organization have the freedom to speculate and dream about what could be, they will continually keep ahead of the thundering herd. But if an organization has tight control and discourages any type of mistake, people will forgo creativity to escape punishment for mistakes.

Mid-life workers can be of great value. Having lived and experienced many situations, they have the potential of being very important. They can avoid major pitfalls. It is absurd to think that mid-life people are only able to follow directions and orders. They live an entirely different life outside the workplace. They are responsible for many intricate aspects of their life. It is sad to think that people can organize large and successful volunteer projects, but when they come to work they punch a time clock and do exactly as they are told. This is a waste of human potential, which can be put to better use within the organization. Again, after a lifetime of following this routine, workers may have trouble trusting that their ideas are really valued.

American companies are losing out to other countries in innovation. It is unlikely that this is due to a shortage of innovative people. Perhaps because of traditional management, workers who entered the work force with high ideals and creative ideas lost them along the way. Perhaps large organizations militate against creative people. As a result, some of the most successful businesses are small and address specific needs. For instance, a high school graduate looks around and notices the increase in dual-career families. He also realizes that many of these families have pets and yards. So he comes up with an idea. He begins a business, "Pooper Scoopers." Within a very short time he has so much business he has to hire additional workers. He saw a need for a service, and he filled the gap. Two mid-life women who enjoy cooking decide to open a catering business with a twist. People call before leaving for work in the morning and order from a menu of three or four entrees. On the way home, they pick up a home-cooked meal for their family. People with ideas are available. The question is how to tap those ideas within large organizations. Mid-life workers have had experience and opportunities to continue to hone their skills. Rapid changes can make it difficult to keep abreast in every aspect of the job. One of the ways this can be addressed is through continuous, lifelong learning. Although this has been utilized to some extent in the past, it is now becoming more important.

CONTINUOUS LIFELONG LEARNING

The need for continuous learning across the life span has been recognized by adult education specialists. They have defined the adult learner as one who has been out of the formal learning environment for three or more years. Studies conducted using adult learners have found several characteristics. Mid-life workers who return to school want to increase their job skills, learn new techniques for handling life's changes, and enhance their own sense of self. These remain rather consistent until later in mid-life, when there is a slight change toward learning for the sake of learning and a pursuit of leisure activities for later years.

Many institutions are involved in lifelong learning. The obvious ones are colleges and universities. Those not so obvious are libraries, extension services, clubs, organizations with a particular interest, and businesses and industries. Adult learners who enroll in colleges and universities are interested in the credit hours that accompany the learning. They want or need these to further their careers. Business and industry have provided continuing education to retrain workers for new jobs or for new innovations in current jobs. Professional lifelong learning has also been around a long time. Most professions expect their members to gain a certain number of continuing education credits to maintain licensure. Others require a continual updating so that members can continue to be current.

As people move through their middle years, they return to formal institutions of learning to broaden their knowledge base, to seek education and training that will lead to a change of careers, or to avail themselves of the liberal arts. The number of mid-life women returning to school after completing their "mothering" duties is increasing. These women have decided that they want to make a different life for themselves, and one way is to be educated or trained. They are marvelous students because they possess a great urgency to succeed. Mid-life women have some clear-cut goals and objectives they want to reach. They also feel that, with their experience, they have a great deal to offer the world of work. Often the world of work does not agree. Because of traditional recruiting and hiring practices, some very talented women are overlooked in the workplace.

As the baby boom gives way to the baby bust, colleges and universities are finding their enrollment shrinking. As a result, they have begun courting the adult learner market. Many such institutions have a greater number of adult learners enrolled than traditional students. One of the problems that occurs is that the instructors have not changed their teaching techniques to take into consideration the adult learner.

The Adult Learner

Since business and industry are involved in reeducation and retraining, they too need to become familiar with how adults learn. For the most part, we teach the way we were taught. This can be disastrous when dealing with adult learners. Knowles (1970) led the way in determining how adults learn. His observations are important for everyone who professes to teach adults. His first observation is that most adults learn in a self-directed manner. They do not sit in classrooms and listen to a lecture, do the work required, and profess to have learned. Most adults recognize what it is that they need to learn. They seek out ways and places that will give them what they need, and then they do it.

Second, adult learning is influenced by individual experience. Younger people learn more abstractly, a result of not having the experience necessary to relate the learning. Adults learn through analogy. The more often the instructor can take a new concept and relate it to something within the learner's experience, the more quickly the adult will learn the new concept. For example, say you want to teach a group within the work force the concept of teamwork. You are interested in getting them to participate in a team approach on a particular project. Part of the learning experience can be to have each member of the group relate an experience where two or more heads were better than one. It might be necessary to prime the pump by giving an example.

Characteristics of Adult Learners

Adults are not passive in learning situations. At the beginning, they may seem to prefer learning through the use of a lecture, but this is often the result of early conditioning. Lectures were how most mid-life people learned during their formal education. It is important to begin to expose them to hands-on learning situations. This allows them to apply life and work experiences when learning new information or skills. Eventually, as they become confident in their own abilities, they will come to prefer this approach. Research has shown that most adults prefer to take an active role in their own learning. They know best what they need. They have little time or patience when they are forced to sit through lectures on concepts that they have already mastered.

Timing is very important. Adults learn best when they are faced with particular life situations that move them to seek specific answers. This is described as the moment of the "aha"—when they suddenly understand. Sometimes we cannot wait until adults are at that point. The teaching experience needs to include measures to move adults closer to recognizing their needs.

Learning, for adults, is problem oriented. It is not unusual to find workers who have no or poor problem-solving skills. Those who do not have these skills will usually do whatever someone tells them. If no one tells them, they search until they find someone. The following example illustrates the principles outlined above. This can be used as a working example if one of your tasks is to ready a group of workers to begin working within a team environment.

The Team Approach

Your family has sufficient savings to take one vacation this year. Both spouses and the three teenagers have different ideas about where to spend the vacation. Mom wants to go to New York to see a couple of shows and shop. Dad wants to fish. Sean, age nineteen, wants to go sailing. Julie, age seventeen, wants to meet a famous movie star and check out some modeling opportunities. Ben, age fifteen, wants to swim at the seashore and meet girls.

There are several ways to resolve this issue. Dad can say: "I am the boss. We are going to rent a cabin in northern Minnesota and fish." This is one management style. Or, Mom and Dad can confer and decide that they will rent a cabin within a resort area in Colorado. Mom can shop and attend the Shakespeare festival. That is another management style. Or, Mom and Dad can say that it is one of the children's turn to pick the vacation spot. The child who has satisfied the family's picture of what a child should be is rewarded and gets to pick the spot. That is another management style. Or everyone can be given the task of locating a place where each family member can do some of what he or she wants to do. A week is allowed to research the problem. The family meets, hears all of the possibilities, and records the pros and cons of each. They then, either through consensus or by a vote, choose one.

Let's throw in one more chink just to make it interesting. Suppose that Julie doesn't do her homework. She wants what she wants and won't co-operate. If she doesn't get her way, she has decided not to go on that vacation. She will pout until everyone gives in and does it her way. The family that chooses a team approach but has a member of the team who refuses to cooperate has another problem. Each of you has already decided what you will do about Julie. The response you have depends on your typical response to problems.

After all workers are given the opportunity to relate how they approach and follow through on team decisions, they are then asked to evaluate the outcome of the team approach. They are next asked to think through the same problem using a top-down approach. Again, they evaluate the possible outcomes. Although this exercise may take some time, it is a hands-on approach that provides food for thought. It is then your job to move from this example to the one at hand within the work environment. You will have holdouts like Julie.

If the team approach is to work, all members must be committed to the concept. The time to weed out those who cannot adjust to another style of decision making is as early in the change process as possible. These people also need to know changes will take place. They need to be presented with their options. They will then need to make a choice. Hard-core resisters may have to choose to look for work within another organization. Although this seems harsh, allowing them to remain unchanged within the current organization could lead to more difficult problems in the future.

Part of the continuous lifelong learning involves training. This training can involve skill development or enhancement of people skills. The example given above can set the scene for the trainer who is involved in teaching team building.

TRAINING

Some organizations hire trainers. Often it is the responsibility of human resource specialists to identify the needs of workers. They then become involved in selecting the appropriate training. They may also do the training if it is within their area of expertise, if they have the time, and if they are expected to do it as a part of their work load.

There are times, however, when outside trainers are needed. If this particular task falls under your domain, here is some information you might find helpful. When trainers are hired from outside the organization, it is important to know whether they are able to quickly discern the dynamics of the organization. Ask for references from other companies that have used their services. Check these references carefully. Training companies need to market themselves to survive.

One of the strengths of a good trainer is the ability to convey a positive message. There are people who talk well, but fail to deliver an adequate product. Know what kind of training you want. Do you want someone versed in organizational development, or are you more interested in human resource development? Some people are better able to work with managers, and others are more competent in technical training. It is important to know what you need and want. Then, if you are hiring consultants outside of the organization, make sure that they can meet your objectives.

A good example of the need for care in hiring outside consultants can be seen in the following scenario. Mr. Smith, the human resource director, found that people were not working together. He decided that the company needed some expertise in team building. He talked with several representatives from a variety of consulting firms that claimed to develop these skills. Mr. Smith hired the ABC firm to conduct the training. After several hours of interaction between managers and the consultants, it became apparent that there was a gap between the expectations of the managers and the information they were receiving. Most of the time was spent talking about how managers interacted with one another and with their employees. After reviewing the afternoon's agenda, the participants found that they were going to experience more of the same.

Since it is easy to confuse team building with teamwork or team training, it is important to continually clarify with the consultants. Words are often used interchangeably. The processes and outcomes are totally different. Mr. Smith was correct in his assessment that the managers needed and wanted more information on team building, but the consulting firm did not make a distinction between team building and teamwork. As a result, money, time, and resources were spent with little return. The consulting firm also suffered. This particular organization would not be able to give them a positive recommendation.

A second reminder involves the role trainers play within organizations. Training is basically a service role. Trainers have to be responsive to the needs of the clients. They also need to be alert to the real objectives of the company. By this I mean, that they need to be able to determine quickly whether the company is really committed to the training. Is your company interested in teaching people within the organization problem-solving skills to deal with short-range or short-term problems? If so, then the trainer needs to know this. Trainers, true to their profession, are interested in teaching skills that go beyond the short-term need. If the training does not satisfy the management within the organization, then perhaps either or both were confused about the purpose of the training.

A commitment to training is mandatory for organizations that plan to be around in the year 2000. Changes in economic, social, and technological advancements underscore the need for continuous on-the-job learning. The trainer becomes the change agent, with training the process by which change is accomplished. Management and workers need to be not only trained to meet existing needs but also prepared to face the changes of tomorrow.

Mid-life workers have experienced change within their lifetimes. Most are able to at least recognize the importance of accepting change. Many have not learned that change is a process. Managers need to be especially cognizant of the change process. If managers do not understand the immediate as well as the long-range steps involved in change, they could abort the process before it is completed. This becomes an important and relevant role for the human resource specialist to play within the organization. It does little good to prepare employees to address change if management does not understand the process.

There are two aspects to remember regarding change. There is the change, which can be best described as a situation. There is also the transition, which is a process. Change can occur rapidly. It is the transition that takes time. An ending occurs with any change. Each person responds to endings differently. You need to be aware of this. When people seem to be disagreeable, impatient, or out of sorts, you can observe whether this is part of the normal change process.

Although people are actually involved in new ways of doing their job, they may still be going through the mourning or loss process that accompanies change. You may recognize symptoms of sadness, anxiety, disorientation, denial, or anger. It takes everyone a different amount of time to finally reach the acceptance stage. Knowing that this is normal when changes are made aids you. Others not involved in the change may come to you to complain about their fellow workers, or managers may seek you out. If you are aware, you can reassure them that the behavior is temporary in most cases. All of this information is handy when you or someone within the organization implements a training program.

Emotional Barriers

According to DiMattia, Yeager, and Dube (1989), there are emotional barriers to learning. Whether the training is provided by an outside group or done in house, it is useful to be aware of these barriers. Studies have shown that there is a proliferation of training being conducted but that little of what is learned during the training is being transferred to the job. To deal with this fact, you need to pay attention to what the authors call "emotional management."

Negative Emotions. Anxiety, frustration, and defensiveness are some of the negative emotions that employees could feel when requested to participate in a training session. When any negative emotion is present before, during, or after the training, this interferes with the actual learning process. Learning to deal with the various components that make up the change process is crucial. Before teaching or retraining, you may want to set up a short workshop with the sole purpose of identifying emotional responses to change in general and then to the proposed change. All too often, we are not willing to spend more time dealing with emotional issues. It has been proved time and again that the long-term goal is better met when this extra time is included in the training package.

Literacy

In an article entitled "Analysts Worry Literacy Efforts Are Misguided" (1990), reference was made to a basic skills program established about two years ago by Frito-Lay. In the program was Mrs. Albert, forty-nine, who was described as having a high school education. She could read and write, but she lacked math, computer, and communication skills. She had been a potato inspector for twenty-five years. She now needed to be able to read and interpret computer-generated graphs showing whether chips were just the right thickness. The chips had to be cooked to perfection and bagged at a precise weight per bag. If these tasks were not accurately done, the company could lose profits, market share, and satisfied consumers.

The American public still equates literacy with reading and writing. Organizations realize that the term is more expansive and are beginning to realize that the work force needs to increase all skills, from the very basic to the highly technical, if they are to compete in the global economy of the 1990s. Other literacy skills identified in this article include computer literacy, effective communication with coworkers, typing, skim reading, and interpreting complicated written or oral instructions. These skills are best taught within the context of the job being performed.

To test a notion I had, I asked thirty-seven students enrolled in an introductory course how many knew how to use a word processor. The students ranged in age from eighteen to forty-eight years. Only about 10 percent knew how to use a word processor. I had noticed in correcting written work that about 1 percent had trouble writing. The others ranged from passing to very competent. I had also noticed that about 10 percent handwrote their work. About the same percent used a word processor. Most in this particular class were able to follow directions given for the written work. Many times, however, students have to redo assignments because they do not follow directions. Fortunately, our campus has a very effective learning center.

People in the center will read papers and give help in correcting grammar and style as well as in upgrading the quality. They also teach people how to use a word processor. There are several available for students' use. Unless the students are forced to use the service, they ignore it. I no longer intensively correct grammar or style. If students have a problem, they must make an appointment with the learning center before I will accept a rewrite. Beginning with the fall term, all papers must be done on a word processor. Content changes, but skills are always important. If students learn how to continue to learn, to express that learning, they can always master the content.

According to the article on literacy, companies are hiring people to teach their employees who have skill deficits. The trainers use on-the-job examples and relate all learning back to the employee's tasks within the organization. Rather than firing employees who do not have the necessary skills, companies are teaching them. Besides keeping valuable employees, these organizations are also promoting goodwill. There is no price tag on that commodity.

Shortcomings of the U.S. Work Force

Thurow (1990), the dean of the Massachusetts Institute of Technology Business School, predicts that in the next step in the evolution of global companies a world marketplace will take place in December 1992. This is when the European community will replace the United States as the world's largest consumer body. Several shortcomings in the U.S. work force will come to light at that time. Historically, the United States has had more natural resources, more capital, better technology, and a better work force. This combination led to great wealth. Japan has shown that even without natural resources, it runs the best steel industry in the world. Natural resources are no longer a player in this game. In addition, no single country holds the key to technological advances. There is extreme competition. Taking this and natural resources away from the United States, we are left with the work force. According to Thurow, the U.S. work force is in sad shape. He has noted, "It takes twice as long to train an American work

force than a German one, because the U.S. doesn't have the basic skills"
(p. 290). Lacking basic skills and processes to respond without negativity
to the frustrations of the day-to-day interactions on the job costs organizations a good deal of money and customers.

Workers Training Other Workers

The intensity and speed of technological advances have caught a lot of
organizations by surprise. Previously, there was time to train or retrain and
utilize the new skills before major changes happened again. One problem
that is difficult to address in a proactive way is knowing what skills, knowledge, and attitudes will be needed tomorrow. How do companies meet these
demands? One answer is to teach basic skills in adapting to change. There
are similar characteristics within all changes. If people learn to accept the
fact that change is a constant, learn the component parts of change, and
learn how to respond to these components, they are at least even with the
game.

Companies can identify people within the organization who have dis-
played an ability to see that change is necessary, who know almost instinctively what the change involves, and who begin to make the transition
without skipping a beat. These people can be used to work with other
employees so that learning takes place while people are doing their job.
Sometimes subordinates learn more easily form their counterparts. The fear
that accompanies change can be mitigated. Organizations should support
those who need retraining as well as those who provide this service.

Kaye (1989) talks about a group of employees described as "plateaued."
Previously, workers who plateau have been replaced by offering either early
retirement or outplacement counseling. Since there is no one group of characteristics for this group, other solutions need to be researched. There are
those who know that they will not be promoted. They have plateaued. But
because the organization continues to provide retraining and allows room
for individual initiative, these workers continue to be productive. This group
could possibly be used to retrain others within the organization. They have
high morale and experience excitement when learning new skills and processes. These people are often self-starters who make the most of their lives
whatever life gives them. They are creative people who are willing to take
risks. They can look at repeated tasks in new ways. The organization could
benefit by using these people to work with others who don't seem able to
move beyond the negative responses resulting from plateauing.

MENTORING

Mentors have always been part of the workplace. Until recently, this
interaction took place without much notice. The mentor is now receiving

more attention as the composition of the work force changes. Changes that affect mentors are increased competition for promotions, increased numbers of women and minorities, and increased knowledge about mid-life and its particular tasks. Mentoring is one of the ways in which mid-life people can leave a legacy and work toward completing the phase of generativity. Besides assuring some continuity, mentoring passes accumulated knowledge and experience on to the next generation of workers.

A mentor is usually a middle-aged person who has worked in a particular area long enough to know the ropes. This person has gained knowledge about the area of interest, and ways of dealing with others and can effectively pass this on. Therefore, a mentor helps younger workers avoid trouble and provides valuable information about the unwritten rules. Mentors make sure that their protégés are noticed and given credit for their work (Levinson, 1978). In the past, everyone knew that certain people advanced because they had a mentor. Younger workers today recognize the importance of having a mentor.

Mentoring Relationships

The mentor relationship usually develops over time. At least four stages have been identified in the mentoring process. The first is initiation, which usually lasts about six to twelve months. During this time, the employee selects the person, and the two begin to develop their relationship. The second stage, cultivation, can last up to five years. During this time, a considerable amount of time is spent assisting protégés with their occupation. Often, the mentor also becomes a confidant. The third stage is the most difficult. It is usually during this time that the younger person is rewarded with a promotion. Often this promotion puts the person on the same level as the mentor. The younger person now needs to let go of the relationship. It is time to prove oneself without the help of the mentor. The mentor also has to let go at this time. If both are not prepared for the sense of loss and loneliness that is bound to follow, there can be trouble between the two. The final stage is redefinition. Each, having experienced the separation, can reestablish the relationship, but with new rules. At this point they can become friends.

Women probably have a greater need for a mentor than men. They have had less opportunity to learn the rules by which organizations run. They also seem to have a more difficult time finding a mentor. One of the reasons is that there are so few women who are in a position to function as mentors. This is especially true in upper-management positions, where fewer than 7 percent of the work force are women. Women can choose men as mentors, but there is an inherent danger in this selection. Cross-sex mentor relationships can produce conflict and tension resulting from possible sexual overtones. Even though there may be no overt sexual behavior on anyone's part, the relationship still can cause problems within organizations.

Mid-life people can be very effective mentors, since they understand the dream. They are in the process of reevaluating their own dream. Helping a younger person, a new entry person, or reentry person define and work toward fulfilling a dream enhances the mentor's own sense of self. If the mid-life person who has entered the mentoring role is secure and has a good sense of self, the protégé will prosper. However, there are times when middle-aged people take on this role but are not personally equipped to conduct themselves properly within it. At these times, the relationship can be destructive for both persons. The protégé sits at the feet of the mentor; therefore, the mentor has a great deal of responsibility. If the mentor is in any way flawed, this can be passed on as acceptable behavior. It is plain to see that inappropriate values, attitudes, and behaviors can be passed down from one generation to another.

Mentoring as a Mid-Life Task

Mentoring is a mid-life task designed to lead people to a greater sense of generativity. Companies are becoming more aware of the importance of mentoring. In fact, some organizations have looked to the human resource specialist to develop mentoring programs. You have probably known about and been in agreement with the concept. You may also have attempted to develop this type of program. Some of you may also have experienced little involvement on the part of middle and senior managers. Being a mentor takes time and energy. For some people, the reward of seeing another make it within the organization is not sufficient to offset the cost. Jacoby (1989) addresses this issue. He suggests making middle and senior management aware that mentoring is part of their jobs. This can lead to a more successful program. There also needs to be a reward system and an evaluation program. The one being mentored should be evaluated, as well as the mentor. Jacoby's feeling is that companies that are interested in developing internally need to make an investment of people and money. He suggests that mentoring be viewed as would any long-term investment utilizing a similar set of criteria. First, objectives should be set in advance of the experience. Second, there should be measurable criteria for evaluation, and third, rewards should be reasonable and consistent. This is one approach that organization can take to insure that younger members use their talents to the fullest.

In a study conducted by Barnes, Mendelson, and Horn (1990), the following recommendations were suggested. Early face-to-face meetings are essential so that the mentor can communicate caring and accessibility. During the early meetings, ground rules need to be established between the mentor and the protégé. A trust level needs to be felt. A casual "how are things going?" is insufficient especially if no rapport has been built. The protégé also needs to know that the mentor has experienced difficulties and has not always known how to handle every situation.

Criteria for Successful Programs

There are some effective criteria for successful mentoring. The mentor has to have a genuine interest in providing this service and has to be available. Mentors also need to be aware of the company's policies and goals. New mentors gain by spending time with successful mentors.

Once a program is established, it is important that everyone in the organization be aware of the program. Clearly stating how the program functions, its expectations, and its potential outcomes increases the success of the program. Confidentiality, supportiveness, and commitment are important.

Unstructured, naturally formed mentoring decreases employee rejection. Not all organizations are structured so that this can happen. Rather than forgo mentoring, some organizations choose to set up a formal mentoring program. Jacoby (1989) indicated that a formal program promoting the concept of mentoring does profit the organization.

Jaccaci (1989, p. 50) talks about mentoring somewhat differently. He suggests that for the workplace to move ahead, the trainers within the organization must become educators. These people would draw out the best in people and aid them in being creative, inquisitive, and able to take the risks necessary to keep ahead of the competition. But more is needed. The educator then needs to become a "mentor of purpose and fulfillment for individuals, groups, and whole organizations." Jaccaci suggests that more is needed than business mentors, who are not always able to fulfill the traditional mentor role unless they can become more visionary. He calls this needed role the "social architect." The major criterion of the social architect is to have broad-based knowledge and a deep understanding of human nature that encourages individuals to know who they are and what they can become. This intense self-knowledge leads people away from doing what they are told and toward a more contributive interaction. Using their capabilities in concert with the goals of the organization leads to greater fulfillment for individuals and organizations.

Being a mentor takes a special kind of person who is able to tap internal resources for the good of the organization. This is done without harm to the individual. The process is like pruning a tree. The dead weight is cut away so that the tree is more productive and healthier. Not everyone is so secure with themselves that they can elicit this type of growth in others. But without the employees' creative involvement, organizations will not be able to compete. There are those people who want to enrich themselves with creative involvement in their work. They will probably find work that will allow them this opportunity. Those who choose to stay in organizations that work from the obedience mode will die on the vine. It is projected that these companies will also become obsolete and unable to maintain themselves. Everyone who succeeds has a mentor. Companies that succeed have viable mentors working with their employees.

Women and Mentors

The following stages are involved in mentoring women. The first stage is that of observer. The woman observes and relates through attention and emulation on an impersonal level. Because women's career paths are more erratic than men's, women often do not move beyond this stage. Those able to be involved continuously in the work force move to the next level. The woman becomes involved with a mentor, who provides guidance and direction. The third stage is the protégé, where the mentor becomes a sponsor and advocate. The fourth stage occurs when the mentor role dissolves and the two become peers (Bolton, 1980).

Women take more time to identify a mentor. They are interested in finding someone with whom they can interact on a professional level. They choose people who will recognize their talents and abilities and aid them in refining these. Fewer mentors have in-depth experiences with mentoring women because until recently women have interrupted their careers. As more women are dedicating themselves to the development of their own careers, they will seek more long-term mentoring relationships. Until there are sufficient women in positions where they can be helpful as mentors, women will continue to identify men. The ultimate goal of mentoring is that the person who can provide the best mentoring is available. Men will mentor men or women, while women will be available to do the same. This move toward more equality between the sexes on a mentoring level has the possibility of being the most effective means of eradicating some of the sexism that continues to linger in organizations. It may also provide more interaction on a professional level among culturally diverse groups. Racism exists when ignorance prevails. Mid-life people who have previously experienced ageism can be seen as potential mentors for young workers who have the knowledge but lack the experience necessary.

LEARNING ORGANIZATION

The time is right to put in place what Jaccaci (1989) calls a learning organization. Basic to this concept is that in return for employees' loyalties, the organization invests in them. This empowers mid-life employees and allows them to be the best they can be. Because of the competitiveness of a global economy, organizations will need to look toward a continuous learning society within their work force. Retraining will take care of providing the skills necessary. Then learning can take place. Employees will need to be aware of what is going on in the world and in their companies and will need to be astute enough to recognize where the holes are. In a learning environment, people can take the time to think, puzzle, and try out new ways of doing things. Mistakes will be made, but sometimes we learn only through mistakes.

Different Styles of Response

There are different ways to puzzle about a problem or situation. Some people will want to experiment. The human resource specialist may recognize that something isn't right within a particular unit (Kiechal, 1990). If that human resource specialist is an experimenter, different combinations of people and tasks will be tried until one works.

Other people use the technique of exploration. They don't know where they will find themselves at the end. They look at their assumptions, test them, and try them again. Explorers don't want easy answers. They want to see if the solution lies within the larger picture. They are not afraid to admit that their basic assumptions need changing.

The visionary is another very important type to have around. Visionaries look at wanted outcomes and then attempt to create innovative ways to achieve the long-range goals. Modifiers want to alter what already exists. They build on the present to meet the future. There are times when each type is important and times when a combination of two or more is necessary. Having all of these types of people within an organization can present a double-edged sword. Respect for differences will be very important. All types will need the maturity to realize that they seek solutions differently, not better.

The visionary may well be an intuitive person who can see the total picture but doesn't have a clue as to how to get there. The modifier is more of a sensing personality who can pay close attention to detail. Each is definitely needed. If each respects the other, then the job will be accomplished. If each fights for rights to each one's own ideas or domains, nothing is accomplished. Precious time and energy are wasted.

Personality Types

Knowing the personality types of all employees within an organization allows jobs and tasks to be built around the particular personality type rather than people being assigned tasks regardless of how they think or operate. The most creative mind in the world is useless there are people who know how to operationalize the ideas. This is the best argument for the team approach. Each team can be made up of a variety of personality types. Extroverts can easily bring group members together to talk about the problems they are having. Introverts need time to go away and think through the problem. They will then seek out individuals with whom to discuss the problem. Attempting to make extroverts act like introverts and vice versa is deadly. Judgers are interested in the bottom line, whereas preceptors are always looking for new data and reach a decision only when forced. Both are needed on the team. A judger may jump too quickly to a decision, whereas the preceptor will amble along for years, never quite getting to the core of the problem.

Probably the most difficult duo is the feeler as opposed to the thinker. Feelers take everyone's feelings into consideration. They have powerful antennae that can pick up the slightest amount of negativity. They will try to satisfy everyone before they move on. Thinkers, on the other hand, seem cold and calculating. If someone's feelings are hurt, too bad. They don't know when they are too terse, rude, obnoxious, or unfeeling toward others. They rarely have their feelings hurt. More often it is their egos that suffer. Problems that arise from conflicts between these two personality types are the most difficult to deal with because neither knows how the other operates. Service organizations attract feelers. It is not unusual for a whole board of directors of nonprofit organizations to be feelers. They have great sympathy and empathy for the downtrodden. If not checked, they will want to save everyone. When nonprofit organizations don't make it, the reason may be that too many feelers held positions of authority. Then combine a feeler with a preceptor and watch nothing ever be accomplished. Organizations need feelers. They also need thinkers. They need the two to work together and to understand what is different about each type. They can then offset each other in a healthy way.

EARLY RETIREMENT

In the past, early retirement meant that people who were between sixty-two and sixty-four years of age decided to discontinue working on a full-time basis. Recently, early retirement has taken on a different meaning. First of all, the age at which full-time workers are leaving the work force is much lower. Because of buy-out plans and better pension benefits, people are making this decision as early as fifty-two years of age.

Some workers who leave at an early age actually change careers rather than retire. Others, because of layoffs, closings, and other types of displacement, choose to describe themselves as retired rather than without work. The rapid changes within the work force cause employees to become obsolete at a much earlier age. Organizations contribute to early retirement by offering buy-out packages that are difficult to refuse. Some employees know that if they do not buy into the offer, they may still lose their jobs.

With a possible worker shortage, those mid-life people who exited from the work force will find themselves being wooed to return. Hopefully, this change will occur. It is difficult to imagine that mid-life people who choose or are forced to leave the work force in their fifties will have the wherewithal to economically sustain themselves into old age.

Retired Mid-Life People

In a *New York Times* article, Lewin (1990) reported that about 2 million people between the ages of fifty and sixty-four were interested in working. A prevailing myth about retired people is that most retire because of poor health. There is no verification of this, but the notion continues. As the retirement age continues to decrease, the myth continues to prevail. The good news is that the myth is inaccurate. A large pool of nonworkers will be available to return to the work force at a time when organizations will be facing the worker shortage.

Although not all these mid-life people will qualify for the jobs that will be available, there is evidence that about 1.1 million will. Some in this group would be willing to work full time, whereas others prefer part-time work. In either case, they can make a contribution if they return to the work force.

Important Considerations

Through a variety of studies, it has been recognized that people will continue in the work force if they have good working conditions, if their jobs are interesting, and if they enjoy their fellow workers. When any or all of these conditions are lacking, older mid-life people who can financially afford it prefer not to work. They will return to the work force if those conditions are met. Although organizations are going through the transition from an industrial, manufacturing economy to a global, information, and service economy, early retirees may still view the work force as less than desirable.

Life after Work

For many early retirees, freedom from work commitments give them an opportunity to delve into an entirely different life-style. If they are financially secure, they can travel, investigate different types of leisure activities, volunteer, or do whatever they have a mind to.

Before mid-life people choose to retire early, they do need to think through some questions and look at their responses. As a human resource specialist, you may be in charge of or have some connection with potential early retirees. You can use some of the following questions to help these people. It is not necessary that they give you a response. Just presenting the questions will give them an opportunity to be sure they have thought through the decision as carefully as possible.

Loss of Work as a Role. How much does the person enjoy working?

People who like their work and even those who do not, will experience a loss. Those who like working may feel this more intensely. They need to know this is a normal process. People often experience more satisfaction from their work than they realize. There is the socialization factor, the sense of being productive and making a contribution and, of course, the paycheck. When people make the decision to retire, they may block any or all of these possibly important outcomes.

Loss of Identity. Are people ready for the sense of a loss of identity? As workers, their life was structured. They had a reason to get up in the morning. They spent most of their day with at least some semblance of a routine. They may be looking forward to no routine, but after years of living and responding in a particular manner, it can be disconcerting to find that no job also means no routine. Are they ready for this change?

They have also gotten a sense of identity from their fellow workers. In fact, some people without realizing it have developed their friendship and support network around their fellow workers. When they leave the work force, they realize that they do not have other friends. It is difficult to maintain intense relationships with former coworkers who are still employed. There are many sad stories about people who, after retiring, come back to visit and find that they do not have much in common with those who were their closest friends.

Some people do not realize until after they have retired that they operate better when affiliated with an organization. In fact, they come to realize that at times it was because of the organization that they were effective, or happy or content, or productive. How much does this mean to the person considering early retirement?

We are more aware of these circumstances causing problems for men because historically men made up the majority of lifelong workers. Even though the problems were known, it was difficult to talk with men about these issues because men tend not to want to discuss things they perceive as so personal. As more women work longer periods within the work force, it is becoming more evident that they too experience losses when they permanently move out of the work force. Those women who have husbands are thought to be able to move into the housewife role without a problem. What is happening is that they too are experiencing major transitions.

Another Career. Some people decide to leave the work force while they are in their fifties. They often do not consider that because of longer life spans, they could be retired for as many as twenty or more years. This could easily be translated into a sufficient number of years spent in another career.

When people lived only to an average age of sixty or sixty-seven years of age, they had already lived most of their life when they chose to retire at age sixty-five. With the life span of seventy-eight to eighty or more years of age, different factors enter into the equation. First and foremost is the financial consideration. Two serious questions need to be addressed: "If you retire today, will you be able to maintain your life-style? If so, for how many years will this be possible?

A second consideration is that of leisure time. People often have plans for all the things they are going to do when they retire. This can include home maintenance, travel, fishing, or any of the leisure-time activities they didn't have time for when working. They need to ask themselves how long it will take to complete those chores around the house. Where do they want to travel and for how long? What will they do when they either can't afford or no longer want to travel? How important is fishing in the overall scheme of things? Even avid fishermen can run into problems. Those who live in certain parts of the country will be able to fish only at certain times of the year. What will they do during the other part of the year?

Planning. Oftentimes people think that they have planned for their retirement when they have taken a look at and done something about their finances. However, this is only a small part of the planning process. Men have a shorter average life span. If they are married, have they and their wives looked at the time when the husbands will no longer be in the picture? Have they made decisions about housing, the part of the country in which they want to live during retirement, the health changes that are part of the normal process of aging, and their own approach to retirement? What happens when the husband decides it is time for to retire, but his wife is just getting started in a career? He wants to live at the lake, which is thirty miles from town. She wants to continue to live in town and work. If the couple hasn't talked over their plans and made changes as each of them changed, there can be some unhappy moments.

Although you will not be able to give those people considering early retirement many, if any, specific answers, you can provide an important service by asking the hard questions. They will do what they want to do, but hopefully because you took the time to ask the questions, they may do it more thoughtfully. This is just one of the many roles human service specialists play within an organization. As you read on, you will again be reminded what an important role you play.

THE ROLE OF THE HUMAN RESOURCE SPECIALIST

Because organizations not only are made up of people but also produce goods and services for people, those people who interact most directly are the human resource specialists. Your major concern is people. As you have surmised from reading this book and other materials, your task is far from simple.

Every organization has an established human resource policy. Whether the policy is written down or handed down by word of mouth, it contains certain goals and objectives. These goals and objectives flow from the overall goal, purpose, and direction of the organization. It is your responsibility to integrate these within the work force. Chances are you had no input in the construction of this policy. You were hired to implement. There are several problems inherent in this situation. First of all, policies dealing with people are based on values. Usually they reflect the values of the people setting the goals and objectives. A second problem is that because individuals differ so greatly, values and goals are sometimes inconsistent.

For instance, the company may favor personal initiative. Zack, who works in public relations, reports to Jason. Zack's perception of the way that Jason handles the job is that Jason makes his own decisions based on the information given him. When Jason is on vacation, Zack is put in charge. The company is about to announce a new product. The news media receives a tip and has asked Zack for an interview. Based on his perception of how Jason operates, Zack grants the interview and discusses the new product. The news media does its job and releases the information to the public. Zack is summoned by the vice-president for production. The company is not at all happy about the premature story on the product. Through a harrowing experience, Zack discovers that Jason always checks with whatever department head is in charge before he goes ahead with his public relations releases.

Though the company supports initiative, it also has certain rules about what initiative is appropriate. Policies can conflict. Luckily Zack learned a valuable lesson without losing his position. The company was willing to recognize that when values or goals are inconsistent, it will have to give in one direction.

Traditional Tasks

You are probably responsible for all policies that deal with human beings and their productivity. Among these policies are those that address vocational skills, which include those necessary to perform the occupational role; labor market skills, which include those necessary to be able to function effectively in the labor market; and finally behavioral skills, which include the development of attitudes and behavioral patterns consistent with the requirements of the organization.

Investment in Human Resources. Your major task is to insure that the employees hired by the organization work at peak performance. People employed by organizations represent an investment. Traditionally, people were seen as an investment that profited the organization. Little attention was paid to viewing workers as a two-sided investment. Now, the company's investment in the people is becoming more of an issue. Workers know that there are two sides to the investment proposition. They are beginning to assert themselves. Companies that are used to viewing workers only as benefiting the company will find themselves experiencing difficulty in the area of human resources.

Human Capital Investments. Traditionally, education was viewed as the major type of human capital investment. Parnes (1984) suggests that several other areas now are being identified, including training programs, health, and relocation. Companies need to take all of these into consideration when hiring people. Employees are looking at the broad range of investments made by an organization when considering entry, reentry, or job moves.

Human Resource Specialists' Response to Present Conditions

Coates, Jarratt, and Mahaffie (1989) provide several recommendations that can aid human resource specialists in meeting the needs of the 1990s and beyond. The first is for the human resource specialist to take a more active role in corporate strategic planning. This makes a lot of sense. As mentioned previously, human resource specialists often inherit goals and the policies needed to implement these goals. With the rapid changes beginning to occur within corporations, these goals can quickly be outdated. This is especially true if the human resource specialists' main concern was the short goal. As in a variety of occupations, paperwork can overshadow any creative planning. Unless an organization is large enough to employ a network of people within the human resource unit, human resource people may have to commit all of their time to putting out brushfires and doing the paperwork.

The second recommendation for human resource specialists is to integrate international assignments into their careers. This may not be possible within all corporations or businesses. It is important that human resource people are well versed in a variety of cultures. Knowing several languages would also be helpful. With the amount of racial tension and discrimination present in the United States, it is difficult to imagine that achieving this goal will be easy. Perhaps a way to finally decrease antipathy toward minorities is involvement in a culturally diverse work force. Exchanging workers from various countries could create a more accepting attitude. Organizations make changes in attitudes toward their workers because of economic stresses. Perhaps the same strategy can be used in relation to discrimination.

A third recommendation for human resource specialists is to have an understanding of not just their own area but of other parts of the company as well. The more people know about the total organization, the more they can appreciate the complexities. This applies to all workers, from maintenance people to computer people to those at the highest level of authority. It has been suggested that by the middle or end of the 1990s, robots will be used to do much of the repetitive work of organizations. Rather than see this as a major threat to jobs, human resource people can begin to work with employees to discover the types of jobs that will be created.

Human resource specialists need to maintain a public profile. Sometimes people in this unit are seen simply as the person who has the financial issues relating to the employees' pay, compensation, and medical and retirement benefits. If the unit maintains too low a profile, the corporation can decide to hire outside consultants to pick up the people interaction. Continuity and presence would be lost.

Be visible and get involved in any major changes that the organization undertakes. Most changes require before-and-after services for employees. Providing these services can enhance the status of the human resource unit. Design teams that incorporate various talents and skills so that corporate heads, management, and subordinates feel that there is always someone with whom they can confer, This can also move the unit from a static or reactive posture to a more proactive stance. Human resource units can be a model of teamwork. Sometimes it is helpful to keep a running log of the process of building the team and putting the concept into operation. Remember, the definition of *team* is the involvement of different learning, thinking, and personality styles.

Characteristics of Different Thinking Styles. There are four different styles that respond to the four quadrants of the brain, often referred to as brain dominance. The particular explanation used here is based on the work done by Browning Group Training and Development Consultants (1985). First of all, no one operates completely out of one particular quadrant. Usually, several quadrants operate simultaneously. On the other hand, one quadrant generally dominates.

Those people whose dominant styles in the left cerebral are interested in facts. They are the analyzer/producers. They follow strict schedules, judge quality of time by the quantity of material produced, want facts and figures to support the issues, and prefer oral directions. They are valuable to the team because they analyze ideas to determine their merit. They are the ones who ask, "What is the rationale behind the idea?"

The left-limbic-oriented employees are interested in form. They are the organizer/implementers. They plan ahead for the next day, month, and year. They read in detail, do not like mistakes, and prefer their directions in writing. Their value to the team is that they keep everyone on track and also implement the ideas. Their question is, "How does this idea apply to our situation?"

The right-cerebral employees are interested in the future. They are the risk takers. They can be described as the visionary ones. They work to the last minute and appear to take less time in completing a task. They prefer pictures or maps for direction. Their value to the team is that they are creative. They see things that others don't see. Their question is, "How can we look at this problem in a different way?"

The final quadrant is the right limbic, which involves feelings. These people are the humanists. They measure in terms of how something affects others. They coordinate tasks through others. They prefer to give and get directions through the use of personal experience. Their value to the team is that they work to achieve a comfortable interpersonal bond among team members. Their question is, "What do you think of the idea?"

This is a very brief overview of an important concept. Packets of information are available, and consultants are also available to deliver workshops and training on this concept for people within organizations. Another consideration is the concept of personality styles. On close observation, the personality types mirror somewhat the types of brain dominance. Human resource specialists can provide a positive service to the organization by introducing these two concepts in tandem. Many so-called personality clashes are really just differences in thinking and working styles. The better teams encompass at least one of each type and educate the members of the team on the differences.

Human resource specialists can be very helpful when major changes such as mergers, acquisitions, or downsizing are being enforced. If they know the company and the employees, they can run interference, ask appropriate questions, and provide insights and plans that could make the changes less traumatic.

Measure potential behavior. This is part of the same type of outcome achieved when building teams. By using materials available, human resource specialists can contribute to better matches between people in a unit and people who will perform particular jobs most effectively.

Just a word about how the brain communicates. Left-cerebral thinkers use facts to illustrate points. Things are presented very matter-of-factly. Emotions are expressed abstractly. There appears to be little or no emotion regardless of the situation.

Left-limbic thinkers ask questions that have answers: Who? What? When? They speak in sentences and paragraphs. They even complete sentences and paragraphs and are very concrete in speaking.

Right-cerebral thinkers ask questions that lead to other questions: Why? How? They tend to speak in phrases and often stop in mid-sentence, thinking others know what they are talking about. They are very abstract in speaking and use metaphors and musical words.

Right-limbic thinkers are very expressive. Their faces are animated. They use expansive, nonverbal gestures. They like to use stories to illustrate points. You will often hear them talking out loud to others or themselves while attempting to learn or understand new information.

Do you recognize yourself in any of these groups? What about the person you have just about given up on? Personality conflicts are often the result of different styles. Learning and appreciating the differences among people are more than half the battle. When this is accomplished, time and energy can be spent attending to the job at hand.

FINAL THOUGHTS

A wide variety of topics has been covered. Many of the topics may not have been new to you. You have probably heard them before, countless times and in countless ways. The following humorous account may summarize best.

Gladys and Jake are talking in the nursing home garden. Jake says to Gladys, "I'll bet you don't know how old I am." Gladys answers, "I'll bet I do." Jake says, "Bet you don't." They go back and forth several times. Finally, Jake says, "Prove it." Gladys replies, "Okay, take off all of your clothes." Jake does this. Gladys looks him up and down. She then says, "You are ninety-two years of age." Jake is surprised. He asks her how she knew that. She replies, "You told me yesterday afternoon."

With all of the day-to-day activities, life's little surprises, and our desires to meet our dreams, we often forget what we know. Others come along, put the information in a new package, use different kinds of examples, and before we know it, we are saying, "I knew that."

Bibliography

Analysts worry literacy efforts are misguided. (1990, July 8). *Omaha World Herald*, p. G-1.

Barnes, A. K., Mendelson, J. L., & Horn G. T. (1990). Structured mentorship for new employees: A case study. *Journal of Applied Business Research*, 5(1), 74–77.

Baron, J. N. & Bielby, W. T. (1985). *Organizational barriers to gender equality: Sex segregation of jobs and opportunities*. In A. S. Rossi (Ed.), *Gender and the life course*. New York: Aldine.

Beattie, M. (1989). *Beyond codependency*. San Francisco: Harper & Row.

Belasco, J. A. (1990). *Teaching the elephant to dance: Empowering change in your organization*. New York: Crown Publishers.

Bolton, E. (1980). A conceptual analysis of the mentor relationship in the career development of women. *Adult Education*, 30(4), 195–207.

Bradshaw, J. (1988). *Healing the shame that binds you*. Deerfield Beach, Fla.: Health Communications.

Bridges, W. (1980). *Making sense of life's changes: Transitions*. Menlo Park, Calif.: Addison-Wesley.

Browning Group Training and Development Consultants. (1985). *Rediscover your brain*. Englewood, Colo.: G. Browning.

Butler, R. N, & Lewis, M. L. (1982). *Aging and mental health*. St. Louis: C. V. Mosby.

Carnevale, A. P., Gainer L. J., & Meltzer, A. S. (1988). *Workplace basics: The skills employers want*. Alexandria, Va.: American Society for Training and Development and the U.S. Department of Labor.

Coates, J. F., Jarratt, J., & Mahaffie, J. (1989). Workplace management 2000. *Personnel Administrator*, 12, 51–55.

Cole, D. (1988, May). Fired, but not frantic. *Psychology Today*, 22, 24–26.

Crino, M. D., & Leap, T. L. (1989). What managers must know about employee sabotage. *Personnel*, 66(7), 31–38.

Deutsch, C. H. (1990, April 29). Why women walk out on jobs. *New York Times.*

Diamond, M. A., & Allcorn, S. (1990). The Freudian factor. *Personnel Journal,* 69(3), 54–65.

DiMattia, D. J., Yeager, R. J., & Dube, I. (1989). Emotional barriers to learning. *Personnel Journal,* 68(11), 86–89.

DiPrete, T. A., & Soule, W. T. (1988). Gender and promotion in segmented job ladder systems. *American Sociological Review, 53,* 26–40.

Downs, A. (1971). *Urban problems and prospects.* Chicago, Ill.: Markham.

Equal Employment Opportunity Commission. (1990). Guidelines on discrimination because of sex. *Federal Register, 65,* 676–77.

Erikson, E. (1950). *Childhood and society.* New York: Norton.

Fitzgerald, L. F., & Hesson-McInnis, M. (1989). The dimensions of sexual harassment: A structural analysis. *Journal of Vocational Behavior, 35,* 309–26.

Forward, S. F. (1989). *Toxic parents.* New York: Bantam Books.

Freudenberger, H. J., & Richelson, G. (1980). *Burn-out: The high cost of high achievement.* Garden City, N.Y.: Doubleday & Company.

Friday, N. (1985). *Jealousy.* New York: Bantam Books.

Friel, J., & Friel, L. (1988). *Adult children: Secrets of dysfunctional families.* Deerfield Beach, Fla.: Health Communications.

Galagan, P. A. (1989). Growth: Mapping its patterns and periods. *Training and Development,* 43(11), 41–48.

Gayle, M. (1990, January). Toward the 21st century. *Adult Learning, 1,* 10–14.

George, L. K. (1982). Models of transitions in middle and later life. *Annals of the American Academy of Political and Social Science.* Beverly Hills, Calif.: Sage.

Gill, A. (1989). The role of discrimination in determining occupational structure. *Industrial and Labor Relations Review,* 42(4), 610–23.

Golden, K. M. (1989). Dealing with the problem manager. *Personnel,* 66(8), 54–59.

Gould, R. L. (1978). *Growth and change in adult life.* New York: Simon & Schuster.

Gray, W. A., & Gray, M. M. (1986). *Mentoring: Aid to excellence in education, the family, and the community* (Vol. 1). Radnor, Pa.: Uncommon Individual Foundation.

Hickman, C. R. (1990). *Mind of a manager, soul of a leader.* New York: Wiley & Sons.

Huszczo, G. E. (1990). Training for team building. *Training and Development Journal,* 44(2), 37–42.

Jaccaci, A. T. (1989). The social architecture of a learning culture. *Training and Development Journal,* 43(11), 49–51.

Jacoby, D. (1989). Rewards make the mentor. *Personnel,* 66(12), 10–14.

Jaques, E. (1965). Death and the midlife crisis. *International Journal of Psychoanalysis, 46,* 502–14.

Johnson, W. B., & Packer, A. E. (1987). *Workforce 2000: Work and workers for the 21st century.* Indianapolis, Ind.: Hudson Institute.

Jung, C. G. (1983). *Modern man in search of a soul.* New York: Harcourt Brace Jovanovich.

Kalish, R. A. (Ed.) (1989). *Midlife loss: Coping strategies.* Newbury Park, Calif.: Sage.

Kandel, W. L. (1988, Winter). Current developments in employment litigation. *Employee Relations, 14*(3), 439–51.

Kaye, B. (1989). Are plateaued performers productive? *Personnel Journal, 68*(8), 57–65.

Keiffer, S. (Ed.). (1984). *The aging employee.* New York: Human Science Press.

Kelley, C. M. (1988). *The destructive achiever: Power and ethics in the American corporation.* Reading, Mass.: Addison-Wesley Publications.

Kiechal, W. (1990). The organization that learns. *Fortune, 3,* 133–36.

Knowles, M. S. (1970). *The modern practice of adult education.* New York: Association Press.

Knox, A. B. (Ed.). (1979). *Programming for adults facing mid-life change: New directions for continuing education* (Vol. 2). San Francisco: Jossey-Bass.

Kram, K.E. (1988). *Mentoring at work.* Landham, Md.: University Press of America.

Lerner, H. G. (1985). *Dance of anger.* New York: Harper & Row.

———. (1989). *Dance of intimacy.* New York: Harper & Row.

Levinson, D. J. (1978). *The season of a man's life.* New York: Knopf.

Lewin, T. (1990, January 28). For the workforce: 2 million who would quit retirement. *New York Times.*

Matejka, J. K., & Dunsing, R. J. (1989). Managing the baffling boss. *Personnel, 66*(2), 46–50.

Middelton-Moz, J., & Dwinell, L. (1988). *After the tears.* Deerfield Beach, Fla.: Health Communications.

Nakken, C. (1988). *The addictive personality.* San Francisco: Harper & Row.

Neugarten, B. L. (1968). The awareness of middle age. In B. L. Neugarten (Ed.), *Middle age and aging.* Chicago: University of Chicago Press.

Nollen, S. D. (1989). The work-family dilemma: How HR managers can help. *Personnel, 66*(5), 25–30.

Pace, L. A. (1989). Employee assistance when managers are substance abusers. *Personnel Journal, 66*(2), 28–34.

Parnes, H. S. (1984). *Peoplepower.* Beverly Hills, Calif.: Sage.

Peters, T. (1987). *Thriving on chaos.* New York: Harper & Row.

Robinson, B. E. (1989). *Hidden legacies of adult children: Work addiction.* Deerfield Beach, Fla.: Health Communications.

Rubin, L. B. (1979). *Women of a certain age: The midlife search for self.* New York: Harper & Row.

———. (1983). *Intimate strangers: Men and women together.* New York: Harper & Row.

Scarf, M. (1987). *Intimate partners: Patterns in love and marriage.* New York: Ballantine Books.

Schaef, A. W. (1986). *Codependency misunderstood, mistreated.* San Francisco: Harper & Row.

———. (1987). *When society becomes the addict.* San Francisco: Harper & Row.

Schaef, A. W., & Fassel, D (1988). *The addictive organization.* New York: Harper & Row.

Schlossberg, N. K. (1987, May). Taking the mystery out of change. *Psychology Today, 21,* 74–75.

Simmerly, R. (1990). Stratonomics: Developing new leadership skills. *Adult Learning, 1,* 19–22.

Smith, C. C. (1990). *Recovery at work: A clean and sober career guide*. San Francisco: Harper & Row.

Snyder, C. J., & Barrett, G. V. (1988). The age of discrimination in employment act: A review of court decisions. *Experimental Aging Research, 14*, 3–47.

Survey of U.S. Merit Systems Protection Board. (1988, Aug. 1). Reported in *U.S. News & World Report, 56–58*.

Tavris, C. (1989). *Anger: The misunderstood emotion*. New York: Simon & Schuster.

Thomas, J. (1982, Nov.-Dec.). Mid-career crisis and the organization. *Business Horizons, 25*, 73–78.

Thurow, L. C. (1970). *Investment in human capital*. Belmont, Calif.: Wadsworth.

———. (1990, July 18). '92 predicted to expose workforce. *World Herald* (Omaha, Neb.).

Trachtenberg, P. (1988) *The Casanova complex*. New York: Poseidon Press.

U.S. Census Bureau. (1985). Current Population Series, P-60#154.

U.S. Department of Commerce. (1986). *1985 statistical abstract of the United States*. Washington, D.C.: U.S. Government Printing Office.

U.S. Department of Labor, Office of the Secretary. (1989). *Older worker task force: Key policy issues for the future*. Washington, D.C.: U.S. Government Printing Office.

———. (1989). *Workforce quality: A challenge for the 1990s, Secretary Dole's agenda for action*. Washington, D.C.: U.S. Government Printing Office.

Viorst, J. (1986). *Necessary losses*. New York: Fawcett Gold Medal.

Wellman, D. T. (1977). *Portraits of white racism*. Cambridge: Cambridge University Press.

White, W. L. (1986). *Incest in the organizational family*. Bloomington, Ind.: Lighthouse Training Institute Publication.

Winnicott, D. L. (1965). *Collected papers*. New York: Basic Books.

Woods, M. P., & Flynn, W. J. (1989). Heading off sexual harassment. *Personnel, 66*(11), 45–49.

Yoder, B. (1990). *The recovery resource book*. New York: Fireside, Simon & Schuster.

Index

About the Author

SHIRLEY A. WASKEL is Professor of Gerontology at the University of Nebraska, Omaha. Her interest in mid-life issues has led her to serve on task forces and advisory committees, develop dozens of workshops and seminars, and become involved in community service for the aging. Waskel is a frequent contributor to periodicals and volumes on gerontology and has recently published articles on ageism, problem solving for the elderly, trends in education for older adults, and parent care. She is a member of the Gerontological Society and the Adult Education Association.